The Entrepreneurial Family

The Entrepreneurial Family

How to Sustain the Vision and Value in Your Family Business

Roger Fritz

Foreword by Gary Player

McGraw-Hill, Inc.

New York St. Louis San Francisco Auckland Bogotá
Caracas Lisbon London Madrid Mexico Milan
Montreal New Delhi Paris San Juan São Paulo
Singapore Sydney Tokyo Toronto

Library of Congress Cataloging-in-Publication Data

Fritz, Roger.
    The entrepreneurial family : how to sustain the vision and value
in your family business / Roger Fritz.
        p.   cm.
    Includes index.
    ISBN 0-07-022592-3
    1. Family corporations—Management.   I. Title.
HD62.25.F75 1992
658'.045—dc20   91-30018
                                                                          CIP

1 2 3 4 5 6 7 8 9 0   DOC/DOC   9 7 6 5 4 3 2 1

ISBN   0-07-022592-3

The sponsoring editor for this book was James H. Bessent, Jr., the editing
supervisor was Fred Dahl, and the production supervisor was Suzanne W.
Babeuf. It was composed in Baskerville by McGraw-Hill's Professional Book
Group composition unit.

Printed and bound by R. R. Donnelley & Sons Company.

For Kate, Nancy, and Susan.
The family I need now and always have.
No husband or father
ever had more support.

For my mother,
who has given new meaning
to the words
independence, determination, and self-reliance.

About the Author

Roger Fritz, Ph.D., is the founder and principal of
Organization Development Consultants. A former corporate
executive and university president, he is internationally
recognized for his consulting work and management
development seminars. Dr. Fritz is also the author of
numerous books in the entrepreneurial field, including the
acclaimed *Nobody Gets Rich Working for Somebody Else.*

Contents

Family Success Scenarios

How other entrepreneurs have grappled with the problems of handling a family business — and won!

Foreword

Nothing will affect our future as much as the rapidly escalating rate of global economic change. As social and political barriers collapse around us, it becomes increasingly evident that the universal language on which our children's future will depend is not English, Spanish, or Japanese. It is the language of *business*.

All over the world, but especially in the emerging economies of the Pacific Rim, Asia, and Africa, normal people with normal ambitions are discovering their potential as trader, manufacturer, entrepreneur. Never will they walk the hallowed halls of Harvard Business School. Indeed, few will attend a graduation ceremony of any kind. And yet, in combination, these family business people will play a greater part in shaping our future than all the world's Big Business.

Roger Fritz—friend, associate, and successful author of more than 20 books on leadership and management—breaks new ground with this latest work, *The Entrepreneurial Family*. I feel sure family businesses around the world will benefit from the insight, eloquence, and down-to-earth common sense bound into this "College for the Family Entrepreneur."

Gary Player

Preface

Is a family business any different from some other kind of business? You bet it is! That's not just because it's smaller. Many family businesses are very large, as a matter of fact, and employ a great many people.

When it's *your* business, you tend to take things more personally. The business takes on a personality; it becomes a part of your life, a part of your family.

Marshall Field, the great Chicago department store owner, liked to greet his customers personally as they entered the store.

Charles Bruning, whose business machines company later was absorbed by Addressograph-Multigraph, knew virtually every one of his employees by their first names, and took daily strolls through the plant, stopping to talk to his employees about their families and their hobbies. At Thanksgiving, the company traditionally gave holiday turkeys to all its employees, and Mr. Bruning usually hand-delivered the birds personally.

Those who work in a family business often tend to take a great deal more *pride* in what they do. In many cases, it's *their* name above the front door. It's *their* product or service being delivered. It's *their* reputation on the line if something goes awry.

It also may be that the family's livelihood depends on their doing their job well. In some cases, the family business may be the only job the owner has ever known. The very livelihood of the family may depend on the owner's ability to manage their business; and indeed, the family's total assets may be tied up in their company in many cases.

Of course, the family business is different from some other kind of business.

A Tradition as Old as Mankind

Once, all businesses were family businesses. Most people lived on farms, raised their own food, and, as often as not, built their own homes.

Farming was the most common form of business. Other folks, however, soon learned that farmers could not provide — or did not choose to provide — themselves with some products, such as shoes and clothing, glassware and pottery, tools and weapons, and some services, like medicine and dentistry, education, and religion. In exchange for those products and services, the farmer was willing to barter surplus food.

The ongoing need to trade one product for another, one service for another, a product for a service or a service for a product brought people together into small communities and gave rise to commerce. Frequently, the church or the doctor or the blacksmith was the nucleus for such a community.

This was the nature of business for many hundreds of years, both here and abroad. Typically, sons learned the skills of their fathers, and if your father were a smithy, you became a smithy. Thus the family business was passed along from generation to generation.

People Were Named for the Work They Did

In the very early days, people were often called by the name of the product or service they provided. If a person worked with metal, he would be called William, the Smith. If he worked with wood, he would be called William, the Wright (or more specifically "the Shipwright," signifying that he worked on building ships, or "the Wheelwright," signifying that he made wagon wheels). If the man made barrels, he was known as William, the Cooper.

Today, of course, those names would be listed as William Smith, William Wright, or William Cooper. The telephone book is full of names like Fisher, Hunter, Tanner, Farmer, Miller, Baker, Cook, Shoemaker, Carpenter, Mason, Plumber, Pastor, Priest, and dozens of others, all similarly derived.

Picture Doing Business Without a Telephone

It is not easy for a young person today to picture what life was like in those older and simpler times. They are accustomed to modern telecommunications, video data displays, and desktop computers. Many of them cannot conceive of an existence without a telephone, a photo-copier, a fax machine, or a personal computer.

It is hard to imagine that today's high-pressure up-scale business atmosphere has really developed within a single lifespan.

Less than 200 years ago, the Industrial Revolution introduced the concept of mechanization, which eventually led to the construction of large plants and factories. That, in turn, led to the growth of large cities and to the formation of huge metropolitan centers.

It was only 100 years ago that manufacturing pioneers like Isaac Singer and Cyrus McCormick introduced mass production methods, and even fewer years since Henry Ford developed the moving assembly line.

Some 80 percent of today's jobs *didn't even exist* at the turn of the century; and just 50 years ago, there was no TV, no electronic computer, no jet airplane, no space shuttle. Doctors did not have antibiotics and could not transplant a heart. People typed on manual typewriters, washed their clothes in wringer washing machines, and quite often, stored their perishable foods in an icebox. Some still used an outhouse, plowed their fields behind a horse or mule, went outside to pump their water, and (the height of luxury for that day!) cooled off by sitting in front of an electric fan.

Still, the family business held on and prospered.

Things Are Different, But Are They Better?

Things are different today, of course. Thanks to another kind of revolution — the Education Revolution — it's no longer possible for parents to provide children with a suitable education on their own. At first, a little learning in readin', writin', and 'rithmetic was all that was required. Then it became a grade school education, a high school diploma, a college degree, and now a graduate degree.

The development of large corporations with national and multinational markets, networks of interlocking companies, millions of dollars worth of plant and equipment, thousands of employees, and an unbelievable diversity of highly technical products and interests has produced a totally new era in business. Things will never be the same again. The rules have changed.

An Old Game, Played by New Rules

Even the definition of business has changed. Once, a person's *occupation* and *business* were the same. Not anymore.

Today, business is the process of managing one's assets, whatever they may be—real estate, machines, money, personnel, patents, copy-rights. All of these are "assets" to be maneuvered like pieces on a check-erboard in performing today's fast-paced business.

Examples

If you cut pieces of cloth to a specific pattern and sew them together to make a fine suit, that's not your business. That's a craft, which we call tailoring. Today, one does not have to know how to thread a needle in order to operate a clothing business.

If you use wood, glue, nails, a few screws, some hinges, and an assort-ment of tools to fashion a kitchen cabinet, a table, or a dresser, that's not your business; that's carpentry. One does not have to know how to run a lathe in order to manage a furniture manufacturing business.

If you plow a field, cultivate it, sow some seed, fertilize, irrigate, weed, and harvest a crop, that's not your business; it's farming. The movers and shakers in today's agribusiness don't have to drive a tractor and may not be able to tell a turnip from a rutabaga.

So today's business is not carpentry, it's not tailoring, it's not farming, it's not building a better mousetrap. It is the process of managing one's assets. One can always hire carpenters, plumbers, tailors, and farm-hands. What one must learn to do is to manage whatever assets the com-pany has available, and do so in a way that will cause the company to prosper and to grow.

A Matter of Flexibility and Timing

As an example of the old company that learned how to accommodate change, consider Studebaker.

Studebaker once made stagecoaches. The automobile put the stage-coach out of business, but Studebaker did not go out of business. In-stead, it began to make automobiles. Those who ran the company sim-ply changed the way in which they managed their assets. Instead of folding up when it could no longer sell any stagecoaches, Studebaker began to produce another product, and continued to prosper for many years thereafter.

Most of the business failures today stem from a general misunder-standing of what the company's business really is.

Learn the Rules, Ease the Pressures

The rules are no different in a family-owned business, but the pressures certainly are.

When errors are made and money is lost, it is less distressing to know that the loser is a nameless, faceless shareholder than someone who is a close relative.

It is much more difficult to answer to the members of one's family than to a board of directors comprised of strangers.

It is easier to confess failure to a someone you barely know than to someone whom you know, love, respect, and live with.

The pressures of managing a business on the threshold of the twenty-first century are tremendous. Companies are plagued with new and ever expanding concerns about taxes, government regulations, foreign competition, unions, rising costs, and declining profits. Stress has become a malady as prevalent as the common cold.

For everyone engaged in the operation of a family business, those pressures—that stress—can be particularly severe.

The purpose of this book, therefore, is not to help you become successful in your business. Other books promise to do that. Instead, it is our purpose to help you cope with the variety of difficult situations that you encounter as you strive to run the family business.

Our belief is that your ability to do so, if not critical to the success of the business, most certainly will enhance everyone's enjoyment of it—especially yours.

Acknowledgments

This project was born when I realized that many of my entrepreneurial clients were experiencing mixed blessings in dealing with their family relationships. Since then, I have become convinced of the need for a single book that focuses on the delicate and usually frustrating relationships between business and family priorities.

The person whose help has been most significant by far is Don Young. He, too, has lived through many of the trials and tribulations covered in a variety of business settings and has keen insights into resolving problems in practical ways.

I am also grateful to my editor, Jim Bessent, for his candid and useful suggestions; to my agent Patricia Haskell for believing in my idea and advocating it, and to my secretary, Pat Williamson, for her patience and willingness to be a sounding board and buffer throughout the process.

Roger Fritz

1

Family Businesses: The Sweet... and the Sour

A good friend of mine—a notorious cynic—argues that "most people" (his words) do not like to work but do so only as a matter of necessity.

He also maintains that "most people who do work" will do only as much work as necessary to retain their jobs.

Further, he says that "most people" want more money, more company-paid benefits, and more time off, but they do *not* want more work, harder work, or more personal responsibility.

If my friend and I disagree over these and a number of other business-related issues, it is probably because we view them from different perspectives. My friend has spent his entire career at the management level of a major international corporation. I have spent a large part of my career working with large corporations too, but I also have spent a substantial amount of time working with small and medium-sized companies, many of which are family owned and operated.

Different Strokes for Different Folks

Family businesses impress me the most—especially those that are just getting started. No laggardness there!

I have seen men and women work 10- and 12-hour days to get a new business going. I've seen them work six and seven days a week, put in overtime on holidays, skip vacations.

Someone Has to Shoulder the Load

No shirking their responsibilities, either. Each customer was too important to them to allow for any sloppiness or poor performance. If customers weren't satisfied, they'd do almost anything to see that they *were* satisfied!

I've seen entrepreneurs of all ages give up the security of well-paying jobs, abandon their pension rights, and even mortgage their homes to get their businesses started. And what did that entail?

- Leasing or buying office space
- Acquiring equipment and materials
- Hiring and training employees
- Doing everything, in short, that other people (or perhaps entire departments) used to do in the companies that they had just left!

Is *this* "shunning responsibility"?

_____ **FAMILY SUCCESS SCENARIO 1** _____

CARL KARCHER ENTERPRISES, INC.
Los Angeles, California

Carl and Margaret Karcher borrowed $311 on their automobile in 1941, added $15 in cash, and used the money to purchase a hot dog cart in south-central Los Angeles. Their first day's sales amounted to $14.75.

Today, the Karchers control Carl Karcher Enterprises, Inc., with some 470 Carl's Jr. restaurants throughout California, Arizona, and Nevada.

The Karchers' pathway to success wasn't flawless. In January 1987, for example, the company closed 21 outlets in Texas and six in Arizona because of losses due to over-expansion. But the tactic worked, and sales for fiscal 1987 totaled $399.3 million, of which $16 million was net profit.

Now the Karchers' aim is to add 60 to 70 new stores a year, reaching a total of 1,000 by the mid-1990s. Their hope is that 15 percent of the new outlets will be franchises. (Some 70 of the present outlets are franchises, most of them operated by members of the Karcher family.)

Little Today but Large Tomorrow

The Karchers are not unique. I have seen other small businesses grow into large companies, whole new technologies developed, and thousands of new jobs created. (The average Carl's Jr. restaurant operated by the Karchers employs 40 people. Their current 470 outlets provide employment for 18,800 people. The planned total of 1,000 outlets, should the Karchers attain their goal, will provide work for 40,000 people!)

I have seen fortunes made, but I also have seen fortunes lost. People with great dreams have been knocked to their knees, only to get up again and go forth with more determination than ever.

Such is the nature of a family-owned business: people with a strong determination, a fierce self-reliance, a willingness to work long and hard in order to achieve their goals.

The greatest innovations for new jobs, technologies and economic vigor today come from a small but growing circle of heroes—the small business people, American entrepreneurs, the men and women of faith, intellect and daring who take great risks to invest in and invent our future.

—Ronald Reagan
President of the United States

Few of those about whom President Reagan spoke consider themselves "heroes," and their goals are seldom grandiose. A little restaurant...a corner bake shop...a sporting goods store...a travel agency...a small manufacturing company.

Their objectives: more opportunity for self-expression, more control over their own lives, a chance to structure their lives in their own way.

Great Oaks from Tiny Acorns

From such modest beginnings, many major corporations have grown. Indeed, if one delves deeply into the history of virtually any major corporation, one usually will find that it began as a small, family-operated enterprise.

Rudolph Wurlitzer founded The Wurlitzer Company on $700, which he collected, dollar by dollar, sleeping at work in order to save the cost of lodging.

Ford, Wal-Mart, Anheuser-Busch, Mars, Marriott, and many other companies *began* as small family businesses, and are *still* controlled by members of the family today!

Do You Gain Freedom or Get "Locked in"?

My cynical friend also sees "most people" as lazy, unimaginative, uninspired, and lacking in ambition. I see people quite differently.

That is not unusual. Seldom do any two of us think exactly alike about anything. To some individuals, a job with a large corporation means unparalleled security and maximum opportunity. To others, it means having to "play the game" according to someone else's rules, having to engage in office politics, and constantly having to face the fear of transfer or of being laid off whenever times get tough. These are not "adventuresome" folks.

To many other people, having one's own business—being "one's own boss"—equals greater personal freedom, more opportunity for self-expression, and a great deal more self-determination when it comes to guiding one's own future.

To be sure, having a business of your own is not for everyone. Where some people see opportunities, others see headaches.

What are the pros and cons of having your own business?

More Freedom of Choice

When you have a business of your own, you have many options that may not be available to the average person who works for somebody else.

- You may not be tied to a nine-to-five workday, for example, or a six-day work week.
- You may be able to take a longer lunch or an occasional day off.
- You get first choice as to when you will take a vacation.
- If you need more income, you can give yourself a raise.
- If there's a chore to be done, and you don't want to do it, you can assign it to someone else.
- You may be able to work closer to home, thereby avoiding long, tiring commutes.

But can you?

Ideally all those things would be true when you work for yourself, but we do not live in a perfect world. In actuality things seldom work out the way we would like—especially when we are talking about a business that is young and struggling to get established.

- Instead of working nine-to-five, you may find yourself working from six in the morning to ten at night.

- Instead of working a six-day week, you may find yourself working *seven* days a week.

- Instead of long lunches, days off, and posh vacations, you may find yourself eating brown bag lunches or none at all—and skipping your vacation entirely.

- If money gets tight, you may decide to forego your own salary in order to pay the other expenses.

- If an employee gets sick, you may find yourself doing his chores as well as your own, including the most unpleasant ones.

As "the boss," you bear the ultimate responsibilities. There are many things that you simply cannot delegate.

Is Family Labor a Help or a Hindrance?

In a family-operated business, family members can provide a good source of labor. Fluctuating labor demands often create a shortage of personnel one day and a surplus the next, and the ability to call in your spouse or your children as the need arises can be a tremendous advantage.

This built-in "labor pool" also offers a number of other advantages:

- It is expandable and retractable, limited only by the number of children, nieces and nephews, aunts and uncles, cousins, and other family members that you have available to call upon.

- When one individual is busy, generally another available person is not.

- Somewhere within the family, there's probably somebody who has the particular skill or experience that you need—bookkeeping, legal, sales, and so forth.

- Although these individuals are not "permanent" members of your staff, they will acquire enough experience over time to be looked upon as "permanent part-timers."

- Since this help is "family," there should be fewer personality conflicts in the workplace than you might experience with outsiders.

- Outside help is expensive, particularly temporary help. In many cases, members of the family—especially one's own spouse and children—are happy to work for far less.

■ And finally, there is the excellent argument that, by working in the family business, children are preparing themselves for the possibility that, one day, they will take it over as their own.

Again, however, we're talking about ideal circumstances. In the real world, there usually are other things to be considered.

Some of the Drawbacks

First, the work must be something that the members of the family are capable of handling. Obviously, many jobs require skills and experience (in some cases, perhaps even a license) that the members of your family do not possess. If the business is highly technical, therefore, the home-grown "labor pool" may be less useful.

Second, the family must *want* to help out or they may be more of a nuisance than an asset. Spouses and offspring generally have agendas of their own, and your business—no matter how vital it may be to the family's finances—may not be a top priority of theirs. Often, having no help at all is more valuable than having help that is unwilling, unenthusiastic, antagonistic, careless, or resentful.

Third, the family's willingness and availability to work may not coincide with your needs on the job. The timing may be all wrong. Suppose, for example, that you need your son's help at precisely the same time that the football coach is selecting the team's quarterback—a position that your son has coveted since grade school. If your son helps you, he may lose his chance to play quarterback; if he doesn't, he may feel that he's let you down. The potential result: A serious personal and family conflict could arise.

One Must Be Sensitive to the Family's Feelings

One of the major differences between working with members of the family and working with "outsiders" is that one must be uncommonly sensitive to the moods, needs, and desires of the family.

If you should cross an "outsider," he or she may complain or even quit; but as annoying as it may be to have to replace a disgruntled employee, difficulties within the family can be far worse. A salesperson, a mechanic, or a bookkeeper can be replaced; a spouse, a parent, a child, or even a more distant member of the family cannot.

Interpersonal relationships are extremely important in a family business. If an individual tries to impose his or her values too strongly on another member of the family, the results can be disastrous.

If relatives are to build and maintain a strong, loving, and respectful relationship, everyone must understand that both *business* and *family* priorities are important, and that both must be considered. When that occurs, some compromise or alternative usually can be found, and the situation can be worked out to everyone's satisfaction.

It also is important to realize that conflicts of this sort do not necessarily indicate a lack of family support. In the example where a son is caught between his desire to play quarterback on the school football team and his desire to help out in the family business, having to make one choice over the other is purely a matter of poor timing. Under other circumstances, the son might be eager to help out; but in this case, he might be forgiven if he is less enthusiastic because his decision might cause him to forfeit a long cherished goal.

In any event, such differences between a parent and a child—between one set of priorities and another—should not be blown out of proportion. If a child is not enthusiastic about the parent's field of business, the parent's work ethic, or the parent's apparent unwillingness to *seek another solution* to the problem, that does not mean that the child is not proud of the parent or supportive of the parent in all other respects.

In such a situation, the problem, after all, is the parent's, not the son's. From the son's point of view, a request for him to help out in the family business and thereby lose the opportunity to play quarterback on the school team could very well be seen as the *parent's* failure to support *him*, rather than the other way around.

Most people will agree that maintaining a happy family atmosphere should take precedence over problems in the workplace.

Your Family's Support: Built on Marble or on Sand?

The family can and should provide a great deal of support to the individual "carrying the load" when a family business is involved.

True, it is more rewarding to create and maintain a successful business of your own than it is to simply bring home a weekly paycheck. There is a strong sense that what you are working to achieve is for the benefit of the *family*, not a General Motors or a U.S. Steel or some faceless horde of stockholders.

Still, there are many times when the pressures mount, when all the odds seem to be against you, when you wonder if it's really worth all of the aggravation, and it's *then* that the support of your family has the most meaning.

When other members of the family have had an opportunity to work in the business and have gained some first-hand knowledge of how it runs, there is more likelihood that they will be understanding and supportive when things go wrong. But even when they have not, it is important that they are sensitive to the daily pressures of running a business and that they do all they can to support and encourage the individual(s) who are doing so for their common good.

Some people argue that this internal support structure stems from an entrepreneurial "it's us against them" attitude. I disagree. I have seen no evidence that entrepreneurs have a more defensive attitude than anyone else.

I believe that *all* supportiveness, regardless of the occasion, stems from a strong sense of caring; but I also believe that much of the support that is demonstrated within an entrepreneur's family is the result of the pride that is derived from knowing that they are *producers* within their communities and not *consumers*. That is, the entrepreneurs have the feeling that they are making their own way, contributing to their communities and not just taking advantage of whatever resources someone else has provided.

The following example illustrates this point very well.

Communities Are *Sustained* by Their Businesses

My family and I once lived in a community that was heavily populated with executives who were associated with a large corporation that had its headquarters nearby. These were successful people, accomplished people, people who had, in many cases, "made their mark" on life.

The best known and most highly respected family in the community, however, were the Johnstons. They owned a retail store in town, employed a lot of the local teenagers, and could always be counted on to participate in a worthwhile community event. There was a Johnston Street in town, a Johnston Park, and a Johnston wing on the public library.

The Johnstons were aware of their position in the community, and justly proud of their reputation—even though many of their corporation-executive neighbors lived in fancier houses, enjoyed more exciting vacations, drove bigger cars, and took home much heftier paychecks.

The Johnstons were extremely supportive of each other, but they were also extremely supportive of their community. It wasn't "the Johnstons *against* the town" but "the Johnstons *and* the town." Their business did not divide the Johnstons from the community; it united them with the community.

This sense of being a part of the community seems to be much stronger among entrepreneurial families than it is among the population at large. It is, in fact, part of the cement that binds communities together.

The Family Can Be a Source of Business Capital

Quite often, one of the more important advantages of operating a family business is the opportunity to obtain needed capital from other members of the family. Parents, grandparents, brothers and sisters, aunts and uncles, cousins, and inlaws frequently have the means—and the willingness—to provide funding for your business, even when such funding is not available elsewhere.

A bank loan usually entails the preparation of numerous documents, the approval of a loan committee, a lengthy wait while that committee comes to a decision, and then—if one is successful in receiving the loan—the payment of heavy interest on the loan until it is paid off.

Not so when borrowing from a relative. If the funds are readily available, it's often possible to get your loan immediately. On a short-term loan, you may not be asked to pay any interest at all; on a loan of longer duration, the rate of interest asked is often far less than a bank would charge.

Even if you pay the same rate that a bank charges, you have the comfort of knowing that the interest is enriching an accommodating relative rather than the shareholders of the bank.

Nobody knows you better than a relative. Nobody is more likely to invest in your intangible attributes, such as honesty, reliability, and the capacity for hard work, than a relative. Nobody is more apt than a relative to gamble on a dream ... an idea ... an unproven quantity.

Also important, at times, is the willingness of a relative to invest in your business without asking for anything more in return than a promissory note. No need to sign over your house as collateral. No need to surrender a piece of the business in exchange for a loan. No need to line up any cosigners. Often, a simple handshake may be enough.

There are situations in which relatives have mortgaged their homes to provide start-up capital for a promising entrepreneur. There are others in which siblings have advanced the entrepreneur his projected share of the family inheritance so that he could start a business. And there are situations in which a child has been allowed to borrow against the parents' insurance in order to raise some needed business capital.

Opportunities for Women,
Minorities, the Young,
and the Old

For large segments of our society, a family business is particularly appealing. These include women, minorities, and certain age groups, such as those below 30 and those over 55.

While equal opportunity laws and various laws prohibiting sex and age discrimination have had some effect on the ability of these people to get and retain worthwhile jobs, it can be argued that the greatest opportunities lie with those who are able to go into business on their own.

Indeed, many local, state, and federal agencies have regulations that require the utilization of *small* businesses and of *minority* businesses whenever possible.

In the *True* Spirit of Women's Lib

It has been said, with a great deal of justification, that the real road to women's liberation is the *economic* road. If women are financially independent, there are no barriers that they can't overcome, either on the job or in the home.

One way toward financial independence for many women is the entrepreneurial route. Upward mobility in one's own business is limited only by one's own skill, daring and aggressiveness. Here are some relevant facts:

- Two to three times as many women as men became business owners between 1977 and 1983 (Source: The U.S. Census Bureau).
- One-fourth of all self-employed Americans are women, a fraction that will double by the year 2000 (Source: The U.S. Census Bureau).
- There are 3.5 million women entrepreneurs in the country (Source: *MidAmerican Outlook*, a business publication).
- New businesses operated by women are twice as likely to survive to their fifth birthday than those operated by men (Source: A University of Tulsa study).

In 1986, women landed $1.6 billion worth of government contracts, ranging from ship repairs and foundry work to management consulting and janitorial services. That figure was up $300 million from the year before.

More Freedom for Minorities, Too

From the standpoint of minorities, the government estimated that 600,000 of the 15 million small businesses in America in 1986 were owned by minorities. That figure doesn't even include the tens of thousands of part-time, unlicensed "cottage industry" businesses that are not reported, as such, in the government statistics.

When It's Your Own Business, Youth Is No Handicap

There is no way of knowing how many young people (under the age of 30, to set a demarcation point) have found success more quickly by going into business for themselves than by starting at the bottom of the corporate ladder. There are, however, some outstanding examples:

_____ FAMILY SUCCESS SCENARIO 2 _____

BALLARD DESIGNS, INC.
Atlanta, Georgia

At the age of 29, Helen Ballard entered a home design contest sponsored by *Metropolitan Home* magazine. Part of Ms. Ballard's entry was a photo showing a dining room table that she had designed—a base of plaster dolphins supporting a glass top. The magazine article resulted in 500 inquiries from people who wanted to buy the table.

Recognizing her opportunity, Ballard sold her condominium to raise capital; designed additional tables, statues, and other items made of plaster (but painted to resemble wood); and produced a 20-page full-color catalog. It was the start of Ballard Designs, Inc. in Atlanta.

Since then (1983), Ballard has mailed her catalog to some half-million people twice a year. Sales in 1987 topped a million dollars.

_____ FAMILY SUCCESS SCENARIO 3 _____

TINDER BOX INTERNATIONAL
Compton, California

In a 1985 leveraged buyout, 30-year-old Gary Blumenthal, a former vice president at Foote, Cone & Belding Communications, and his four partners bought a troubled chain of tobacco stores from Imasco Ltd., a Canadian conglomerate. Smoking had lost its popularity, and the chain's sales were falling dramatically.

As president of Tinder Box International (50 company-owned stores and 150 franchises), Blumenthal added gift items—games, leather goods, and collectibles—to the inventory.

By 1987, gifts accounted for 30 percent of the California company's $70 million in revenues, the firm was producing a six-figure annual profit, and Blumenthal was hoping to add up to 200 outlets to the chain.

_____ **FAMILY SUCCESS SCENARIO 4** _____

CHILDREN'S DISCOVERY CENTERS, INC.
Monroe, Connecticut

In 1983, 28-year-old Arnold Diamond and some partners invested $325,000 to form Children's Discovery Centers, Inc., a chain of day care centers headquartered in Connecticut.

Diamond knew that the market looked good. No company dominated the field, and some nine million children under the age of six have working mothers who need help to take care of their children. That figure had jumped to 13 million by 1990.

In 1984, Diamond's company opened its first center. During that year and the one following, the company sought out and bought 17 other centers, acquiring each one for an average of $50,000—considerably less than the $500,000 that it can cost to build a center from scratch.

In October 1985, the company went public. It also used $4 million of its new capital to finance the acquisition of Mary Moppets Day Care Schools, Inc., a company based in Tempe, Arizona with 50 centers and an additional 46 franchises.

Diamond, just 30 years old, was on his way!

_____ **FAMILY SUCCESS SCENARIO 5** _____

I CAN'T BELIEVE IT'S YOGURT
Dallas, Texas

In the late seventies, teenage sister and brother Julie and Bill Brice were working in a yogurt shop. That was the year they became entrepreneurs.

Using $10,000 that had been set aside for their college education, Julie (18) and Bill (19) bought the yogurt business, which they eventually franchised.

Today, I Can't Believe It's Yogurt, the Brice's Dallas-based company, has some 200 outlets, and Julie has bared turned 30!

One's Never Too Old to Earn

While there are no statistics available, there are some excellent examples of people over the age of 55 who, after full careers in other pursuits, have had remarkable success in businesses of their own.

_____ FAMILY SUCCESS SCENARIO 6 _____

UGLY DUCKLING RENT-A-CAR
Tucson, Arizona

After 35 years as an insurance and investments agent, Tom Duck envisioned an unusual niche in the rent-a-car field — a market for older, less attractive cars, rented at a fee significantly lower than the fees that other car rental companies were asking. At 63, Duck formed Ugly Duckling Rent-a-Car System in Tucson, Arizona.

Today, Ugly Duckling ranks fifth in the number of rental locations among the nation's car-rental companies, and it has become an $85 million business.

_____ FAMILY SUCCESS SCENARIO 7 _____

MARKETING SERVICES, INC.
Kansas City, Missouri

Bernard Morgan worked for Hallmark Cards for 25 years before he retired in 1976. Preferring work to idleness, he formed Marketing Services Inc., a company to create and sell promotional products such as bumper stickers, banners, and coffee mugs.

Well past 55, Morgan is now worth $5 million. Of equal importance to him, a company trust account — fully funded in 1987 — will guarantee him $120,000 a year for life.

Small Businesses Will Continue to Increase

One thing is obvious: Corporate mergers, industry cutbacks, foreign competition, job obsolescence, and a number of other factors are going to result in the displacement of more people in the years ahead — plus a commensurate draw-down in the number of jobs for them to move into.

Consider these statistics:

- In the five years between 1979 and 1984, the Labor Department says 5.1 million people, including 500,000 at the management level, lost their jobs. With more recent economic setbacks, including the savings and loan disaster, entire new blocks of middle and upper management personnel are joining their blue collar compatriots in the unemployment ranks.

- During the first five months of 1986, Fortune 500 companies reduced their manpower by over 2.2 million people. Now, much smaller companies also are beginning to realize that it's important, in today's economy, to run "lean and mean." They too are trimming their payrolls. ·

- Ford and General Motors alone cut 20 percent of their white collar workers over the past few years.

- If you now work for a major corporation, in a white collar capacity, the Bureau of Labor Statistics says your chance of losing your job this year is one in ten.

Who can say how many of these people — young, old, women, minorities, and others — will attempt to go into business on their own? Right now, some 600,000 people each year are doing it.

Find a Market, Then Find a Way to Serve It

Another advantage to the family-operated business is often *the opportunity to capitalize on a captive market* made available by a relative. In other words, it may be possible to derive enough income to "underwrite" a startup from built-in customers.

One young entrepreneur, working in the family store, saw her opportunity to go into business — and took it.

The young woman's family had opened a giftwares store that specialized in merchandise imported from abroad. In time, the operation grew from the original store to a chain of five stores. A variety of suppliers were providing their merchandise.

The young woman, daughter of the owner, had worked in the stores since she was a teenager. She knew the stores, their merchandise, and the tastes of the customers. She saw how much business they were giving their suppliers and reasoned that she could start her own company, travel to the countries from which their merchandise originated, and buy the merchandise to supply the family stores.

With the five family stores as a captive market, her business was able to break even at the very outset. In time, she not only replaced some of her parents' suppliers but signed on a number of other customers as well. With the increased volume, her company began to produce a profit, she was able to hire some help and rent a warehouse, and her business was solidly established.

Some Carve off a Piece of the Company for Themselves

The young lady in the previous example saw an opportunity to form a new company that would complement the family business. Howard Brownstein used a different approach, but to the same end.

After working in the family business for eight years, Brownstein bought out one of its divisions in 1985. Three years later, his Peregrine Metals Groups Inc., based in Rosemont, Pennsylvania, was producing $25 million in revenues.

Not Every Dollar in the Till Is Profit

As we said before, operating a business is not for everybody, and a factor that one person sees as a plus will appear to someone else as a minus. Some examples follow.

There Is Pressure from the Inside and Out

If the business is going well, almost everybody will get in line to help you take the credit for it. But when things go poorly, you'd better screw up your courage, put on your thick skin, and get ready for some rough weather! The good decisions, you will discover, are "ours"; the bad ones are "yours."

Pressure from people outside the family is bad. Pressure from the members of your family, the people about whom you care the most, can be worse—almost unbearable at a time when you need their support the most.

- Those who once were the most encouraging can become the most derisive.
- Those who settled for a handshake when they first loaned you money may now badger you for a lien on your house.
- Everyone will be convinced that you could get by with a much smaller car.

Financial setbacks usually are the most stressful, of course, but there are other causes of stress as well.

- Key employees can get ill, quit, or retire.
- Critical personnel may decide to go into business for themselves, taking your best customers with them.
- Machinery can break down.

Is there no relief from such pressure? Yes, but it doesn't come about accidentally. Here are some things that will help keep you sane.

1. *Keep yourself in good physical health.* Nothing will make tensions worse than a corresponding bout with illness.
2. *Make the time to do things that help you to relax.* Play golf, go fishing, watch a ballgame. Whatever helps you to relax will help you to fight off tension.
3. *Set attainable goals.* In other words, don't *look* for tension by setting your goals too high and then fretting over not being able to reach them. You will be amazed at how much you can accomplish if you simply move ahead a little bit each day.
4. *Don't bottle up your concerns within yourself.* Talk to people, especially those whom you love and trust the most. Often, discussing a problem with another party will not only release the tension, but lead to the discovery of an amazingly simple solution as well.

Your Suppliers' Problems Can Become *Your* Problems

If your supplier can't deliver, perhaps you won't be able to deliver. If your supplier's prices go up, you may have to raise your prices. If your supplier's product becomes obsolete, your business may become dated as well.

Perhaps you can't solve all of your suppliers' problems (nor should you) but you can take steps to protect yourself against harm when they do occur. For example:

1. *Insist on a written contract that describes every detail of your arrangement.* Handshakes were OK years ago, but they won't hold up in court today.
2. *Never "lock in" to one source of supply.* Be sure you have a backup, if necessary.

3. *Constantly review the arrangement you have made with a supplier.* Is their product or service the best you can get for the price? Is their delivery prompt? Could you do better elsewhere?

Your Customers' Problems Can Become *Your* Problems

If your customers no longer want, or need, or choose to use your product or service, you and your business can be in serious trouble. If your customer's business declines, your business may decline. If your customers don't pay their bills, you may not be able to pay your bills.

Once again, it is not your responsibility to solve your customers' problems, but you should take some precautions to see that their problems don't become your problems:

1. *Just as you should with your suppliers, you should have written contracts with your customers.* Don't create opportunities for misunderstandings to occur.

2. *Communicate regularly with your customers, especially the major ones.* Then, if trouble does loom on the horizon, you have a chance of learning about it *before* it has a chance to involve you.

3. *Read business and professional journals that will help to inform you about potential problems—yours, your suppliers', and your customers'.* You can get subscriptions of your own, or read the publications in the local library; and don't overlook the financial pages of your daily newspaper.

Outsiders Can Change the Rules

No matter what you do, unexpected changes in local, state, or government regulations, in the local, state or national economy, or in any number of other internal or external factors can cause all your plans to go awry.

You may not see these changes coming, and seldom will you be able to do anything about them, but your ability to cope with such changes will often be critical—and will *always* be stressful.

Here are a few of the things that you can do:

1. *Deal with knowledgeable bankers, accountants, and lawyers, and touch base with them from time to time.* Ask them to alert you of things that you should know.

2. *Belong to any business groups that relate to your field of interest.* These can range from the local Chamber of Commerce to the very

sophisticated international professional societies, and they're all a good means of keeping informed as well as making important business contacts.

3. *Read.* The dozens of available business-oriented publications, including your daily newspaper, will alert you to things that are under consideration and that could affect your business.

4. *When you hear about something that is being proposed, and you think that it is wrong or potentially harmful, make it a point to attend the public hearings and testify.* If you can't do that, at least write a letter to anybody who is in a position to help you fight for your cause.

You Can't Pass the Buck

Being able to "pass the buck" is one of the greatest ways in the world to relieve tension.

"That's the way we've *always* done it," contends Tom, and — zap! — his pressure disappears.

"It's not *my* responsibility," says Dick, and — biff! — the pressure comes off.

"I only did what Charlie told me to do," claims Harry, and — pow! — all of his pressure is gone.

But when you're the boss, there's no one else to blame, no excuse that is acceptable. The responsibility is yours and yours alone. Employees who make mistakes might lose their jobs, but if the mistake is serious enough, the boss can lose the business!

During his presidency, Harry Truman lived by this fact and even made an asset out of it. Prominently displayed atop Truman's desk in the Oval Office was a sign that read:

THE BUCK STOPS HERE.

The same thing applies in every business. It is the result that matters, not who's to blame.

But there are other ways to relieve tension than to pass it along to somebody else. For example:

1. *Accept the fact that you have the responsibility to resolve the issue and do it!* Procrastination only adds to the tension, and turmoil.

2. *If the solution to your problem is beyond your scope, don't make matters worse by experimenting.* Trial-and-error can lead to more problems and bigger problems. Go out and find somebody who can solve the problem for you, even if you have to pay them to do it.

3. *Learn to accept your mistakes and to laugh about your mistakes.* Trying to excuse, apologize or explain an error only increases the tension; it doesn't remove the mistake. And for a real tension-breaker, there's nothing that can compare to a good belly-laugh.

Your Stress Becomes the Family's Stress

Stress can alter your personality... change your disposition... and in so doing, make you a very difficult person to live with. As stress brings about changes in you, it can bring about changes in your spouse and your children as well, and in so doing, it can make them more difficult to live with. As you become more difficult, and the members of your family become more difficult, the tensions at home can increase rapidly, sometimes to explosive proportions.

Stress feeds upon stress, and many entrepreneurs can tell you that business pressures were the direct cause of many marital problems. Unfortunately, a substantial percentage of those situations resulted in divorce, in teenage rebellion, in verbal and physical abuse, and in combinations of them all.

One's ability to cope with stress should be a key consideration when a business venture is under investigation. To paraphrase another of President Truman's favorite sayings: "If you can't stand the heat, stay away from the business."

Business is a gamble in a number of ways. Generally, the greater the gamble, the higher the potential return... but also the higher the potential for stress. Like the person who sits in on a high stakes poker game, anyone who engages in a high-stakes business venture should clearly understand the risks. It is one thing to gamble one's time, one's money, or even one's reputation, but it is quite another to gamble one's health, one's marriage, or one's entire future.

To say "leave your troubles at the office" is much too simplistic. It simply doesn't work that way. Instead, turn that old tune around:

- *Take your work home with you.*
- *Talk about it with anyone who will listen.*
- *Try not to brag too much about your successes, but spill out your defeats.* You will find that most people are pretty understanding, and some may even be able to offer some good advice, given the chance.

In any event, those in whom you confide will feel that you have made them a part of your situation and they will be much more sympathetic than you might imagine.

Always Look for the Negatives
Along with the Positives

The relative importance of these factors—every potential advantage and disadvantage—varies from individual to individual. They also vary in significance according to the size of the business involved, the nature of the business, and even its age. If there is one aspect of being in business that does not seem to suit you, then look twice as hard at the next one because *opportunities do exist* and you do not want to miss out by being overly cautious. Conversely, if everything about the business picture seems to come up roses, then go back and check each factor a second time because *the booby traps are there*. Those who succeed in business are those who are the most skillful in learning were the pitfalls are and how to avoid them.

Chapter 1 Checkup

Self-Guide to Managing a Successful
Family Business

To get where you want to go in business, you must set out on a course that you have thoroughly and carefully laid out for yourself. The following questions cover matters that need to be decided by you and you alone. There are no right or wrong answers, but each question should be carefully deliberated and answered in the best way you know how. Refer to these questions and answers as you continue through this book. More important: Refer to them at the end of 30 days.

1. My top three business goals for this month will be:

(a) _____

(b) _____

(c) _____

Why?

_____

_____

_____

Are these goals reasonable? Yes _____ No _____

Are they attainable?   Yes _____ No _____

2. I will strive to improve myself in the following ways this month:

   (*a*) _____

   (*b*) _____

   (*c*) _____

   Why?

   _____

   _____

   _____

3. How will these improvements benefit the family business?

   _____

   _____

   _____

   How will they benefit my family?

   _____

   _____

   _____

2

The Right Structure Helps the Business *and* the Family

It may not matter very much initially, but eventually the way in which a family business is structured can be extremely important. It is the way in which a company is organized that determines:

- Who the owner(s) are.
- Who actually controls the business.
- How much authority rests with each person involved in the business.
- How the business may be passed on to succeeding generations.

Anything that important deserves more than passing attention, of course.

The government has provided a number of ways in which a business may be organized. Each one has certain advantages and certain disadvantages to the owner(s), and each should therefore be considered fully as a means of being sure that the most advantageous method is selected. If it is not:

- The business and/or its owner(s) may be paying more taxes than necessary.
- They may not be taking advantage of certain tax advantages that the law provides.
- They may be laying the groundwork for future problems regarding control of the business, legal accountability, and how to pass the company along when it is time to retire or an untimely death occurs.

To explore all the possibilities, it will be necessary to view the situation from two points of view: (1) the startup of a new family business and (2) taking over an existing business, whether it has come down through the family or whether it is being acquired by new owners.

Starting a Business from Scratch

In one of my earlier books *Nobody Gets Rich Working for Somebody Else*, I attempted to provide a comprehensive guide for those who plan to go into business for the first time. Without going into nearly as much detail here, it is important to point out that there are a number of advantages to starting a business from the ground up.

The ability to build or rent a facility that is precisely the way you want it

When buying a new business or taking over an existing business, you often discover that you are coming onto the scene at a time when the company has reached certain limitations. It has outgrown its facilities, the building is in dire need of reconditioning, and so on.

Over the years, the refinishing of certain roads—or the construction of new ones, particularly interstates—alters an entire community's driving and shopping patterns. It can also change urban transportation routes, which may make it difficult for customers or employees to get to your place of business.

When you start from scratch, you have the advantage of picking facilities that will be best suited to today's needs.

The ability to equip and decorate the new facility to suit your own needs and tastes

Just as buildings and neighborhoods can become outdated, so can machinery, which can wear out or become totally obsolete as new technologies come along.

Even the general appearance of the place can become outdated. Remember when retail stores had uncarpeted wooden floors and those old-fashioned glass showcases?

When you begin at the beginning, you can get the latest equipment and the most contemporary decor.

The ability to select your own staff

Taking over an existing business, you inherit the existing work force. Sometimes, that's to your advantage; indeed, some businesses are purchased just so the new ownership can obtain the services of the old firm's key personnel.

Sometimes, however, it's not to your advantage. You may be gaining personnel who have "burned out," who no longer make a meaningful contribution to the business, who are overpaid for the work they do, or who are simply filling in time until retirement.

Starting afresh, you can pick your own people and train them to do their jobs as *you* want them done.

The ability to start with a "clean slate"

Moving into an existing business requires a certain learning period. Of course, if the business has been in the family for generations and you have worked there since you were a child, you probably are familiar with most of the situation—but not necessarily *all* of it.

It is amazing how many little things go unnoticed in the course of doing business:

- Why a particular job is handled in the way that it is
- Why a certain supplier has been selected over another
- Why the business banks where it does
- Why some customers are extended credit and others are not
- ... and on and on

If you are taking over an established company, you must learn the answers to all these things. If you are beginning anew, you create your own policies and procedures according to your own preferences. You can start small and grow gradually, without having to digest everything in one large gulp.

The ability to take advantage of certain tax concessions or financial inducements that may be offered by the government

Very often, if a company is considering a facility in a new community, the local, county, and/or state governments will provide the firm with certain inducements to persuade its management to settle there. These inducements can range from providing free land or a free building to the reduction or elimination of taxes for a given period. Some governments have even aided the new company with the training of its employees.

Naturally, Disadvantages Also Exist

While there are many advantages to starting a business from scratch, there also are many advantages to taking over an existing business. Usually, the benefits of taking over an existing business tend to underscore the disadvantages of starting a business from the ground up. Some of those disadvantages follow:

The need for a new business to make its presence known

You cannot automatically assume that a carefully chosen location is going to produce a good volume of business, or that being from a well-known family is enough reason for people to change their customary buying habits and beat a path to your doorstep.

Word of mouth works wonders, but you probably will have to advertise, hold promotional events, participate in trade shows, and do a variety of other things that will call attention to your new company, the field that it is in, and—most of all—its reliability and quality.

The inability to find a suitable site

True, you may not be tied to an old site that no longer meets your needs. On the other hand, it may not be possible to find any other site that (a) is suitable and (b) is affordable.

It is often said that three things are essential in business: location, location, and location. The inability to find a suitable location can seriously hinder your plans. You may even have to consider a location in some other city.

The inability to find and hire suitable personnel

You can't run a business without personnel, and in some areas skilled, reliable, affordable help is not easy to find. When you buy (or take over) an established business, one of the things you acquire is an in-place work force.

The need to train your work force

You would be fortunate, indeed, to hire personnel who are capable of doing your work without receiving any additional training. Often, however, it will be necessary to train them in some manner, even if it is nothing more than to show them how to use the fax machine.

The more technical your business, the greater the amount of training that you will be called upon to provide. In most companies, training is a never ending task. New technologies and new business methods make it necessary for management to teach their personnel how to understand them and put them to use.

Taking longer to "get up to speed"

As hard as you try, getting a new business underway usually is a slow, excruciating process. When you take over an established company, you are more likely to be able to hit the ground with your feet moving.

The lack of an established customer base

Customers are the sum and substance of a successful business. Having an established customer base on which to build is a decided advantage. If you start a business with no customers at all, every one you do get will have to be won over from a competitor, lured to your company through advertising, or attracted by lower prices, exceptional quality, or outstanding service. Whatever your business-building technique, the process is usually slow, costly, and time consuming.

Difficulty in establishing the necessary cash flow

Until your business has been able to establish a certain clientele, it is difficult to establish a dependable level of income. The rent and the utilities must still be paid, the employee payroll must be met, suppliers' accounts must be kept current, and that may mean dipping into your reserves from time to time until a steady cash flow has been developed.

...A myriad of details to handle, from finding a name for your new business to engaging a janitorial service

Only after you have evaluated the disadvantages as well as the advantages will you be in a position to decide which course of action is best for you.

Buying (or Taking over) an Existing Business

Buying an existing business may not be as costly as one might think. On the average, the purchase price of a small business is only in the range of $75,000 to $80,000 — approximately the amount that you would expect to pay for a modest house. And there are a number of good reasons for buying a business that's already in operation.

The ability to study the company's books

As often as not, those who start a new business from scratch are taking a considerable gamble because the business has no history on which to base important decisions. But going into an existing business, the new owner can review the financial records as a guide to such important information as:

- Source and amount of income.
- Cause and amount of expense.
- Stability of cash flow.
- True worth and extent of all assets.

Acquisition of certain legal rights or proprietary technology

Such things as copyrights and patents often are the very basis upon which a business is built.

Xerox, for example, was founded on the basis of a patent for xerography.

Polaroid was founded on the basis of a patent for the Land instant camera.

Charles Kettering's heirs are still receiving income from the royalties on his patent for the automobile self-starter.

The estates of Walt Disney and Jackie Gleason are still collecting on their rights to the creative properties that those two entertainers produced during their lifetimes.

Obtaining the services of certain key personnel

When you acquire a company, you generally acquire its personnel. In some cases, critical personnel are on contract to the firm, and such contracts have considerable value.

An easy example is the acquisition of a professional football team. Such a business depends on the quality of its personnel, and those personnel are all under contract to the team. When you buy the team, you acquire the players' contracts. Without the players' contracts, the team would be worth considerably less—and perhaps nothing at all.

Gaining an established customer base

An established business has an established list of customers, plus a record of those customers' purchases over a period of time. From such records, it is possible to project the amount of future business that the company can reasonably expect to receive from each customer. From such projections, in turn, it is possible to calculate with a fair measure of certainty your production needs, your personnel needs, and so on.

Obtaining a good facility, fully equipped, on a choice site

Obviously, it is no small matter to find a good site for your business, plan the building you want to put on it, erect that building, and then fill it with the kind of equipment and machinery that you need to do your work. When you buy an existing facility, you take advantage of the fact that *somebody else* has done all that work for you.

Other possible benefits follow:

- A site may be irreplaceable because such property no longer is available. For example, many close-in golf courses are completely surrounded by housing, and it would be impossible to acquire a comparable quantity of land in a similarly convenient location today.

- Since prices seem to escalate every year, the equipment and machinery that you can acquire with an existing business—although used—may be of better quality, yet cost less than the products that you would be able to buy today.

- Since you are, in effect, buying used property, you may be able to get a better, larger, more completely equipped facility when you acquire an existing business than you could afford to buy if you were starting from scratch.

Obtaining valuable inventories of products and materials

If you are dealing in a product, it takes time to acquire the materials that you need to work with. It takes even more time to turn that raw material into enough of your product to serve the demands of your market.

When you acquire an existing business, you also acquire its inventories of raw materials and its inventories of finished product. Usually, both are sufficient to keep the company going while you are making the transfer of ownership and getting used to your new role as the head of the company.

Acquiring a solid business reputation

It can take a long time to build and maintain a solid business reputation, but you can buy or take over a company in which the reputation already is established.

Getting an established distribution system

It also can take a long time to line up a productive stable of jobbers, distributors, and dealers. But an existing company may already have a good distribution system in place.

Acquiring established, dependable sources of supply

Knowing where to get the things that you need at a fair price, from a company that can be relied upon for quality, delivery, and dependability, is a long and tedious process. Such sources of supply should already be established in an existing business.

Eliminating a competitor

Not the least of the benefits of taking over an established firm is the fact that, in so doing, you a removing one competitor from the field. As the years go by, you may be able to acquire or merge with other competitors— one of the simplest and most effective means of building a business. But even at the outset, it's a benefit that should not be ignored.

Once Again Consider the Negatives as Well as the Positives

Against the impressive list of benefits for buying an existing business, you must weigh a number of drawbacks. For example, the previous owner might have a good reason for wanting to sell the business, and that reason may not be what it seems. Caution is advisable. So, against the impressive list of advantages to buying an existing business, one should weigh the reasons that it may not be a good idea. Some of those reasons follow.

Run-down or obsolete facility and/or equipment

When you enter an existing business, take a good look around. Be forwarned if the equipment and machinery are obsolete or about to fall apart, if the repair bills to keep them running have become a major business expense, or if the building in which the company is housed is a candidate for collapse.

Inept, poorly trained, overpaid, or unmotivated personnel

Good people are the life's blood of a strong company. If, for whatever reason, the staff at an established company are no longer doing an enthusiastic, productive job, then the company is in serious trouble.

Do you really need that kind of problem?

An unfavorable union contract

Related to the problem just discussed, there is the matter of the company's union contracts. Inept management in years past may have resulted in contracts that are life threatening to the profitability, the cost competitiveness, and the very future of the firm.

Look before you leap.

A poor company image

Past management may have destroyed the image of the company, or at least given it the kind of image that you do not choose to be associated with. True, it is possible to change a company's image. It has been done many times. But large-scale public relations campaigns cost money and take time.

Sometimes, a new management will take the shorter, easier road and simply change the company's name, but that's not always desirable. If a part of the company's commercial appeal is an old, well-recognized name, it might be better to improve the image than to discard the name.

Excess inventory

Overzealous management, sudden changes in the economy, and a number of other factors may have reduced the demand for your product, leaving the company with a large and expensive inventory.

That inventory has cost the firm money, but it hasn't produced any revenues in return. Furthermore, the company is paying taxes on it while it sits in a warehouse. And, depending on the nature of the product, it may be growing obsolete or it may be fading, spoiling, rusting, or drying out, in which case you may *never* be able to sell it, even at rock bottom prices.

Check the books to see where the company's assets lie. If it's in unsold inventory, be wary.

Outdated and obsolete company products

Presumably, you will have a good knowledge of the industry into which you plan to move. If so, you will know whether the company's products are on the cutting edge of technology or whether they are outdated and fast becoming obsolete.

Does the firm have new products on the drawing board that it will be able to put into production quickly?

How does the company's products stack up, overall, against those of its leading competitors?

Bad contracts with the suppliers or customers

Look over the contracts to which the company is committed. Is the company locked in with a particular supplier? Are the terms reasonable? Can you operate profitably under the terms of those contracts? How long do the contracts have to run?

What about the contracts that the company has with its customers? Can you operate profitably under their terms? How long do they have to run?

An obligation to service outstanding products

Generally, a company that produces a product will cover that product with some sort of warranty.

Are the company's products still under warranty? Are those warranties costing the company money? How much longer will those warranties last? Have much investment will you have to maintain in parts inventory to see you through those warranties?

Poorly kept, inaccurate, incomplete, or inadequate records

Take a look at the company's total record-keeping situation. Too often, new management will look only at the financial records and ignore the rest. That is a mistake. Be sure that all of the company's records are in good shape:

Supplier records

Customer records

Patent records

Tax records

Copyright records

... Every kind of record that is essential to the sound, profitable operation of the business

Possible responsibility for the previous management's debts and other legal or financial obligations

Are you absolutely *sure* that you're not inheriting a lot of hidden debts? Lawsuits or potential lawsuits? Other legal or financial headaches that you haven't been told about?

Check it out—fully!

A weak or ineffective Board of Directors

There are boards and there are boards. In many companies, the board is extremely powerful. Is your board strong or weak? Can you get rid of the dead wood on it? Can you see to it that a few of your own people are made members of the board to look after your interests?

It might be well to point out that there is some reason for the previous owner to sell the business. That reason may not always be what it seems. Caution is always advisable.

Franchise or Leveraged Buyout?

Among the most popular means of acquiring an existing business these days are (1) to engage in a leveraged buyout (LBO), and (2) to obtain a franchise.

Take a Ride on the LBO

In a leveraged buyout, a group of investors—usually including some of the firm's key employees—arrange to buy the business from the owner. The investors may gather the needed down payment amongst themselves or they may arrange for additional financing from a bank or some other source. The balance of the purchase price is paid over a specified period from the proceeds of the business.

Franchising—Learning from Others

In many respects, acquiring a franchise can be considered something of a compromise. You are starting from scratch, you really are "buying into" an existing business.

Your particular business may be new, but the products or services of the business are well established. You will benefit from working with an established name and image, and you have the experience of the parent company and the other franchisees that you can call upon.

There are some other advantages to obtaining a franchise:

- The company will help you select a good site and help you design, equip, and possibly build your facility.
- The company will train you and help you to train your staff.
- The parent organization and/or an association of other franchisees will help you to promote your business.
- If you eventually decide to sell out, the parent company will help you find a buyer or possibly even take over your business itself.
- Compared to the 20 percent of all small business that survive their

first ten years, *90 percent* of the franchise businesses manage to do so (source: U.S. Small Business Administration).

Obviously, those who buy a franchise must sacrifice many of their personal prerogatives. The product or service is predetermined. The name of the business already is established. Most of the business procedures have been set, and, by contract, must be followed. Regular reports will be expected, and the parent company may occasionally send an inspector to check over your operations.

In addition to the franchise fee, the franchisee will need money to build or rent facilities to house the business, to equipment it and put in the initial inventory, and to staff it. Most franchises require an ongoing royalty fee that ranges anywhere from 3 to 12 percent of gross monthly sales, and many also charge an advertising fee that can range from 1 to 3 percent.

Furthermore, a good franchise can be quite expensive:

SOME TYPICAL STARTUP COSTS

Franchise	Type of business	Startup cost
McDonald's	Fast food	$500,000
Kentucky Fried Chicken	Fast food	$150,000
Southland Corp.	7-Eleven stores	$53,000
West Coast Video	Video rental	$240–350,000
Hallmark Cards	Card shops	$145,000
Jiffy Lube	Auto lube service	$130,000
Dollar Rent-a-Car	Auto rental	$50,000
Dairy Queen	Ice cream stores	$150,000
Taco Bell	Mexican fast food	$375,000
Pak Mail Centers	Private postal services	$15–60,000
RE/MAX	Real estate	$15–25,000
Hair Performers	Hair salons	$60,000
Dunhill Personnel	Temporary employment	$75–125,000
Merry Maids	Maid service	$12–15,000
Travel Network	Travel agency	$40,000
Mini-Golf	Miniature golf courses	$11–50,000
Fox's Pizza Den	Pizza and sandwiches	$51,000
Kwik Kopy	Printing services	$150,000
Midas International	Auto repair services	$175–206,000

Still, franchising offers enough inducements that it continues to grow in popularity. The U.S. Chamber of Commerce says 352,495 new franchised businesses were started in 1987, producing $171 billion in sales. The year before, there were 317,751 startups with $153 billion in sales. In 1988, over 400,000 franchisees were operating over 500,000 outlets and tallying nearly $640 billion a year in sales. Since 1980, the number of companies offering franchises has approximately doubled.

Almost every conceivable field has one or more franchiser:

Fast foods	Haircutting
Cleaning and maintenance	Real estate
Health and fitness	Ice cream and yogurt
Business services	Home decorating
Auto maintenance	... and on and on

Many now offer franchises abroad as well as in the United States.

For more information on franchises, contact the International Franchise Association, 1350 New York Ave. NW, Suite 900, Washington, D.C. 20005.

Your Choice of Structure: Help or Hindrance?

Whether you start from scratch, acquire a franchise, engage in a leveraged buyout, or simply buy an existing company, one of the first major decisions that you must make is how to structure the business.

There are five basic possibilities:

Sole proprietorship

General partnership

Limited partnership

Closed (Subchapter S) corporation

Open corporation

The following paragraphs will give you a brief overview of each type and cite some of the advantages and disadvantages of each. Naturally, the best approach is to consult a lawyer before you make a decision.

Sole Proprietorships: A Small Business Monarchy

The simplest form of business, a sole proprietorship, actually lacks much structure. It is a true business monarchy. Since they are the easiest and cheapest form of business to get started, however, many family enterprises begin that way. According to Dun & Bradstreet Corp., 250,000 new unincorporated businesses were formed in 1986.

A typical example is Christifer's Plumbing & Heating in Arizona.

_____ FAMILY SUCCESS SCENARIO 8 _____

CHRISTIFER'S PLUMBING & HEATING
Tucson, Arizona

Caral Christifer was one of 7,544 people to take out a business license with the City of Tucson in 1987. He then had some business cards printed and began to look for work. Occasionally, he now takes on a part-time employee.

This is "small business" at its purest. A person decides to enter business, takes out a license, and is on the way. In many cases, the whole process may take less than a day and the whole cost may be nothing more than the licensing fee; in some areas, even the licensing fee may be waived.

_____ FAMILY SUCCESS SCENARIO 9 _____

ADVANCE PUBLICATIONS, INC.
Staten Island, New York

The family-owned Newhouse media empire, headed by brothers Norman (now deceased), S.I., and Theodore Newhouse, started as a sole proprietorship. Five-year-old Norman sold copies of the Bayonne, New Jersey _Times_ on street corners.

In time, of course, the brothers incorporated, enlarging their business empire to include ownership of 29 newspapers, the Random House publishing company, and a dozen magazines, such as _The New Yorker_, _Vogue_, and _Vanity Fair_.

_____ FAMILY SUCCESS SCENARIO 10 _____

THIRD WORLD PRESS
Chicago, Illinois

Another publisher who started as a street corner hawker is Haki Madhubuti, head of Third World Press. In 1966, Madhubuti wrote a 60-page book of poetry called _Think Black_ and paid a printer $350 to produce 1,000 copies of the book for him. Madhubuti then sold the books on street corners in Chicago for a dollar apiece.

Since then, Third World has published the work of Gwendolyn Brooks, a Pulitzer prize winner and Poet Laureate of Illinois, and Chancellor Williams, historian and author of *The Destruction of Black Civilization.*

Most "Cottage Industries" Are Proprietorships

A large percentage of the sole proprietorships belongs to those who are involved in the so-called "cottage industries"—businesses operated wholly or in part out of their owners' homes. These firms participate in a great many fields of business, but they usually are small and they often are only a part-time pursuit rather than the owner's sole source of income. Cottage businesses are inexpensive and easy to organize, there is minimal record-keeping involved, and the owner pays no businesses taxes.

These sole proprietorships, however, present a number of serious drawbacks that are worthy of consideration.

Taxation at a higher rate: All income from the business must be reported as personal income on the owner's annual income tax. Therefore, it is taxed at a much higher rate than that at which business income usually is taxed.

Fewer tax breaks: There are no tax breaks for such things as fringe benefits and insurance, for example.

Greater difficulty in borrowing money: In order to grow, most businesses need to borrow capital at one time or another, and it generally is much harder for a sole proprietorship to get a loan. If the company is incorporated, it can sell stock (give up equity in the business) to raise capital.

Unlimited personal liability of the owner: The owner of a sole proprietorship is exposed to unlimited personal liability. A lawsuit can attach everything he owns, not just the assets of the business. Although insurance is available, it can be very expensive and probably will not cover all of the potential loss resulting from a lawsuit.

Difficulty in building equity for the next generation: When the owner of a sole proprietorship dies, the business is automatically dissolved. What he leaves to his heirs is his personal estate, not the equity in a business, stock in the company, and similar investments.

Generally, a sole proprietorship is an acceptable business structure until the income from the company reaches about $65,000 a year. After that, the liabilities outweigh the advantages.

Typically, a family business will start as a sole proprietorship, but eventually incorporate, as did The Buffalo Exchange.

_____ **FAMILY SUCCESS SCENARIO 11** _____

THE BUFFALO EXCHANGE
Tucson, Arizona

Kerstin Block got the idea for The Buffalo Exchange—a used clothing store where items are carefully marked and as attractively displayed as new clothing—in 1974. Originally, she was the sole employee, and her husband Spencer helped out after hours and on weekends with the bookkeeping.

But as the business grew, Block incorporated, hired a staff and named her brother and sister-in-law to the board of directors.

Today, The Buffalo Exchange operates five stores in two states and can afford to provide paid vacations and health insurance to its 45 employees.

Forming a Team? That's a Partnership

In a general partnership, two or more people join together to conduct a business, and each person is jointly and severally liable for the operations of the business. Individuals, corporations, and even other partnerships may form a partnership.

Internal Revenue Service figures for 1984 showed that there were 16 million small businesses in America and that 1.6 million of them—or exactly one in ten—were general partnerships. Partnerships are almost as easy to form as sole proprietorships. A written agreement isn't even required, although they are strongly recommended. Assets, including cash, business-related deeds, bills of sale, and anything else that the business will need in order to function must be transferred into a partnership.

A partnership also can borrow money.

The partnership becomes a separate legal entity, but it does not pay income taxes. Instead, it computes its annual taxable income (or loss) and files a U.S. partnership tax return with the government. This return allocates the income (or loss) to each partner, who then must report it on his or her individual income tax return.

Like a sole proprietorship, a partnership makes all partners jointly liable for the debts and obligations of the business. A creditor can seek the assets of any or all partners, and any agreement among the partners to share that responsibility, although binding on them, is _not_ binding on the creditor.

TRI-MARK, INC.
Wilmington, Delaware

John Kinch learned what a terrifying situation a lawsuit can become.

After leaving the army, Kinch went into partnership with a friend's father in the operation of Tri-Mark, a Delaware printing firm. Soon thereafter, Kinch learned that the company owed $30,000 to the Internal Revenue Service. Confronted, his partner simply walked out.

Kinch then discovered that the company owed $25,000 to the bank. His ink supplier brought suit against the firm for nonpayment. An office closet revealed five boxes full of additional unpaid bills. And the $25,000 profit shown on the company books actually was a $77,000 loss.

Kinch borrowed money from his family and friends. He prevailed on his suppliers and creditors to grant him some extra time to pay his bills. He pushed his sales force to bring in more business.

Fortunately, Kinch's hard work and perseverance paid off. His company now earns a $500,000 profit on annual sales of $8 million.

Many others have been less fortunate.

Partnerships by Professionals

Partnerships often are formed by professionals, such as doctors, dentists, lawyers, and accountants. This form of business has a limited life, usually specified in the partnership agreement. If any partner dies, becomes incapacitated, goes bankrupt, or simply withdraws, the partnership automatically terminates unless otherwise specified in the partnership agreement.

A partner may transfer his or her interest to someone else or pass it along to an heir at the time of death, unless forbidden to do so by the partnership agreement. A sound partnership agreement should provide for a buyout in the event of a death or in the event the partnership should break up. If that agreement permits the remaining partner(s) the right of first refusal and specifies that the interest in the company cannot be sold to anyone who offers a lower amount, a fair price and a mutually satisfactory buyout generally can be arranged.

For Best Results, Pick Your Partner Carefully

The most important part of forming a partnership is the selection of a partner. Simply because an individual is a close relative does not mean that he or she will be a good business partner, and a *bad* business partner can be disastrous, *especially* if that partner is a relative.

Estimates show that partnerships break up as frequently as marriages — about 50 percent of the time — and perhaps slightly more often. Therefore, the careful selection of one's partner can be extremely critical to a successful business.

Look for a partner who:

- Stimulates enthusiasm
- Stimulates new ideas
- Is easy to work with and is not egocentric, autocratic, or stubborn
- Can offer a different perspective and has complementary talents or experience
- Uses logic rather than emotion
- Shares the same goals
- Is a good team worker

Investigate your future partner carefully. You may have been acquainted since childhood, but you may not really *know* each other. What are your partner's good characteristics, bad characteristics, credit rating, lifestyle? Talk to your would-be partner's friends, neighbors, previous employers, co-workers, and spouse.

Consider working at an initial project on a trial basis. How do you get along while working on it? Do you work well as a team? How does he or she respond to suggestions and react to stress?

Finally, strive to avoid a 50-50 relationship. Titles don't mean much: one can be chairman and the other can be president, but *someone* has to be in charge. Somebody needs to have the authority to break a tie when close decisions have to be made and there is a difference of opinion between you.

Limited Partnership, Limited Liability

In a limited partnership, one or more *general partners* manage the business and are personally responsible for its debts, while the *limited partners* have no role in day-to-day business operations and are liable only to the extent of their investments for the company's financial obligations.

As in a proprietorship, this structure avoids double taxation; that is, the taxation of both the business income and the individual income.

Obviously, the limited partnership offers more benefits to the inves-

tor than to those who want to actively engage in the business. But to that
extent, at least, it is a useful type of business structure whenever the situation fits.

The "Closed" or Subchapter S Corporation

During 1973, according to Dun & Bradstreet Corp., 330,000 businesses
were incorporated. In 1986, 700,000 were incorporated. Corporations
are the safest, generally the most versatile, and therefore the most common form of business structure apart from the sole proprietorship.

Not all new corporations are new businesses. Many are proprietorships and partnerships that have "moved up" to a more sophisticated
structure.

A lot of people incorporate solely for legal or tax reasons.

A number of companies form "subcorporations" under the parent
corporation in order to separate their liabilities.

Survival Tactic

*A large residential builder might incorporate each new project
separately. In that way, each of the other projects—and the parent
company—will be protected in case anything disastrous should occur
on any one project.*

The dramatic increase in the number of firms incorporating each
year also is due, in part, to the huge settlements being awarded in court
cases these days. Everyone is familiar with the high—and ever increasing—cost of malpractice insurance for professionals such as doctors and
lawyers. As a direct result of that trend, increasing numbers of professionals are forming personal service corporations, even though they are
taxed at a flat 34 percent, a full percentage point above the highest rate
assessed against nonincorporated self-employed individuals. In 1986,
the American Medical Association announced that 54 percent of all doctors in private practice were incorporated compared to just 31 percent
in 1976.

A Way to Recover Those Early Losses

The "closed," or Subchapter S, corporation can be a useful vehicle for
getting a new business started. That is precisely why the provision was

put into law in 1958. Under Subchapter S regulations, the company passes all of its gains and losses to the stockholders, enabling the stockholders to use any initial losses the business may incur during startup to offset their earnings from other sources *up to the amount that they have invested in the company.*

Subchapter S corporations may have subsidiaries providing they do not own more than 80 percent of the stock of a subsidiary, and they cannot have more than 35 stockholders.

Subchapter S corporations can be converted to conventional "open" corporations later on, but once that is done you must wait five years before you can revert to Subchapter S status.

The Usual Form of, or "Open," Corporation

Legally, a corporation—even a Subchapter S corporation—is an entity totally separate from its investors. It is responsible for its own bills, files its own income tax returns, and pays its own taxes. It can sue and be sued. It lives on indefinitely, regardless of who its stockholders may be at any given point in time.

The Best Protection Against Liability

The primary advantage to a corporate form of business structure comes from the fact that the owners (stockholders) are fully sheltered from the liabilities of the company. This can be particularly valuable to those who are attempting to build a fast growth company in which considerable risk may be involved.

This is not to say that the people running a corporation are completely absolved of responsibility. Poor management certainly can be sued by the stockholders for malfeasance or nonfeasance. Also, there are very strict restrictions banning "insider" trading—that is, purchasing or selling stock on the basis of secret information available only to an "insider" and not to the public at large.

A corporate business structure offers several other advantages.

1. *Corporations issue stock—actually, shares in the business—that can be sold in order to obtain new capital.* Stock also can be used as security for loans, like cash in arranging a merger, and as inducements in the hiring and retention of key personnel.

A company can sell off some of its shares when the price is high and buy back some of its shares when the price is low, thereby using its own stock as a medium for investment.

2. *Corporations pay lower taxes than individuals.* On the other hand, corporate income is taxed twice—once at the corporate level and again when the profits are distributed as dividends to the stockholders, who pay taxes on them as personal income.

3. *In converting from a proprietorship or a partnership to a corporation, those who own and operate the company are forced into a valuable period of review.* Who really owns what? Who contributes what to the business? Who does what? Who is responsible for what? How should the company's assets be divided?

4. *In a corporation, the ones who run the company may not be the ones who own it, and those who "own" the company may not be the ones who run it.* The head of the firm actually may be an employee, hired by the stockholders to manage the company, in which case the stockholders may have no real input as to how the organization is run day by day.

5. *Corporations offer advantages regarding medical, disability, and life insurance, and advantages regarding a variety of valuable pension plans.* Your lawyer and accountant can advise you about each of those.

A 30-Second Review of Your Organizational Choices

Let's recap the various choices in picking an organizational structure.

Sole proprietorships are useful to individuals who are starting small businesses almost single-handedly and with a minimum amount of capital. The taxes are high, and the personal liability is great.

When two or more people go into business together, the *partnership* can be a useful type of business structure, but it is wise to have a thorough, carefully detailed partnership agreement that sets forth each partner's role. Once again, taxes are high and the personal liability is great.

As soon as possible, a *corporate* business structure is the most advisable. The tax rate is lower and there is virtually no personal liability. At the outset, forming a Subchapter S corporation can be useful because it enables the stockholders to deduct business losses from their individual income taxes. Later on, the Subchapter S corporation can be converted to a conventional corporation, which will enable the firm to raise additional capital through the sale of stock. (Subchapter S corporations can have no more than 35 stockholders.)

Why are we recommending incorporation so strongly? Primarily because we assume that *everyone* who is in business will want their companies to grow, and the corporate structure is the one best suited to growth.

A recent study by Bruce Phillips, of the Small Business Administration Office of Advocacy, and Professor Bruce Kirchoff of Babson College in Massachusetts, indicates that the greatest percentage of business failures occurs among companies that fail to grow. A company that starts with four employees or less and fails to add any employees over the years has only one chance in four of surviving for six years. But if the company that starts with four employees or less can double its number of employees over that six-year span, its chances of survival rise to 65 percent, according to the study.

What the Phillips-Kirchoff study shows is that *growth* is critical to a successful business, which comes pretty close to echoing one of my favorite old adages:

There's only one way to coast — downhill.

Chapter 2 Checkup

How Well Do You Understand Business Organization?

1. Name three advantages to starting a business from scratch.

(a) _____

(b) _____

(c) _____

Explain why each of these is an advantage.

(a) _____

(b) _____

(c) _____

2. Name three disadvantages to starting a business from scratch.

(a) _____

(b) _____

(c) _____

Explain why each of these is a disadvantage.

(a) _____

(b) _____

(c) _____

3. Name three advantages to taking over an existing business.

(a) _____

(b) _____

(c) _____

Explain why each of these is an advantage.

(a) _____

(b) _____

(c) _____

4. Name three disadvantages to taking over an existing business.

(a) _____

(b) _____

(c) _____

Explain why each of these is a disadvantage.

(a) _____

(b) _____

(c) _____

5. Name two benefits derived from forming a sole proprietorship.

(a) _____

(b) _____

(To confirm your answers, refer to pages 34–36.)

6. What are two disadvantages that may arise from forming a general partnership?

(a) _____

(b) _____

(To confirm your answers, refer to pages 38–39.)

7. Describe a Subchapter S corporation in your own words.

_____

_____

(To confirm the accuracy of your answer, refer to pages 40–41.)

3

At Home, Doctor Jekyll; At Work, Mister Hyde

To have both a successful business and a happy family is somewhat like playing Doctor Jekyll and Mister Hyde. In order to establish and maintain a sound, well-adjusted family, one must be patient, understanding, forgiving, and generous (Doctor Jekyll). In order to operate a successful business, one must be self-directed, demanding, and sometimes even relentless (Mister Hyde).

It is nice to think of those with whom you work as an "extended family," and indeed in firms where all of the employees are members of one family, the tendency to treat your staff in a parental fashion is almost inescapable. Yet there are many good reasons to retain a well-defined line between your business life and your home life.

Your House Should Be a Home

The qualities that make someone successful in business also can make that person a horrible spouse or parent—and vice versa.

If you saw the movie *The Great Santini*, or read the book on which it was based, you will remember that the hero was a career military officer who ran his family like a military unit. I have never forgotten a line from that movie which, to me, seemed to sum up the entire plot. The line came from Santini's young son who, having grown disgusted with the G.I. rigidity in the family, finally braced up to his father and inquired, "How do you get out of this chicken s— outfit?"

As the operator of a family business, don't let that happen to you.

Learn to Lead a Double Life

Dealing with members of the family calls for a different approach to authority, discipline, and responsibility than dealing with an employee. Each situation should be treated differently, even when the employee happens to be a member of the family.

On the job, unsatisfactory workers can be demoted, have their salaries docked, be made to work overtime, or even be fired, even if they are a spouse or your children. But at home, you can't demote or fire one of your children. You can't dock your spouse's salary or make your spouse work overtime.

When a spouse or a child is actively engaged in the business, interpersonal relationships become more difficult. The key to maintaining domestic tranquility involves *everybody's* ability to understand that they *all are living double lives*. Everyone must realize that the home is the home and the job is the job.

A Change of Hats ...
A Change of Titles

At home, family titles (husband, wife, son, daughter) describe the relationships among the various members of the family. At work, titles (supervisor, bookkeeper, clerk, dispatcher) apply to the job and to the relationships that exist among the people there.

A businessperson does not need a spouse at the office. A businessperson needs a bookkeeper. And if both roles are filled by the same person, then both the businessperson and the spouse should keep those two roles within their proper context.

Members of the family must learn that a spouse ceases to be a spouse, and a son or daughter ceases to be a son or daughter, when they are on the job. Family relationships must be left at home, and each member of the family must be willing to become "just another employee" as far as the family business is concerned.

Your Priorities Will Set the Tone

To successfully handle a "double life," one must give the matter a little thought, and consider such priorities as:

- Which title would you covet the most: "Top Business Executive" or "Spouse/Parent of the Year"?

  Really? Don't answer this question too quickly. Nobody is looking over your shoulder; be honest with yourself.

- How important to you is your family? Your work?

  Don't flit past this question, either. Dig down; take a good look inside yourself.

- Do these two sets of values conflict with each other? How can they be made to complement each other?

  Answer these two questions, always keep the answers in mind, and you will be on your way to health, wealth, and happiness!

- What kind of relationship do you want to have with your spouse? With your children?

  Do you have a plan, or are you just "playing it by ear"?

- What are your personal long-term goals? Your spouse's? Your children's?

  Write down what you think your spouse's goals and your children's goals are, and then ask them to write down their goals. Comparing the two sets of answers might be revealing!

- How does your work conflict with those goals? How does it complement those goals?

  This can be an interesting exercise. Have you given any thought, for example, to when you would like to retire, and to what you would like to do when you do retire? The sooner you have a plan, the better.

Use Your Plan as a Guide ...

It's a good idea to write down your goals and objectives, and to refer back to that list at regular intervals. It will help to keep your life, and your career, on track.

Such a list should never be considered "chiseled in stone." Times change, circumstances change, and so should your goals in life. The sooner you recognize a major change in direction, and take the suitable steps to accommodate it, the better off you will be.

Referring to your targets in life can be particularly valuable in times of crisis. Handling a crisis often is much easier when you have a clear understanding of where you *are* and where you *want to be*.

as a Topic for Discussion...

Have your spouse take the same self-examination that you have taken above. Don't "coach." Don't "suggest." Let the responses be genuine and spontaneous, not the ones that your spouse *thinks you want to hear*.

Now sit down and compare your answers. Where they agree, you have no problems. Where there are differences, talk them out. See how you can accommodate your spouse's needs, when they differ from yours, and how your spouse can accommodate yours.

Next, it's the children's turn. Ask them to take a simplified version of the test. Again, let the process be natural and spontaneous, not something that they're doing just to please you. If you have more than one child, deal with each one separately. This is a one-on-one exercise, not group therapy. Go over each child's answers with him (or her). Explore what feelings they're really trying to express. If any of their goals appear to be out of line, see if you can't get them back on track—but gradually, rationally, and without threats. (This is a good, nonthreatening way to explore your children's values, and you should take advantage of it.)

... and as a Teaching Tool with the Children

Discuss your own self-evaluation with each of the children. The children will understand you better if they can learn "what makes you tick."

When your goals and theirs agree, express how much that fact pleases you. When your goals do not agree, let them know that you appreciate their candor and approve of their individuality, that it's OK to be different, as long as their objectives and their means of reaching them are worthwhile, and that you intend to help them throughout life to the best of your ability.

(This also may be a good time to point out that *your work is what makes it possible for you to provide that help when they need it.* Later, when your work may appear to interfere with something that the children want to do, this talk may make them a little more understanding of the situation.)

If you and the members of your family clearly understand each other's priorities, you can avoid many conflicts later on.

Flexibility Is Needed at Home

In the closeness of a family business, good communication takes on increased importance. Members of the family must learn to talk to each other often and openly. This will help to prevent major misunderstandings down the road.

When you are an employee in someone else's company, your family usually is less involved in your work. But when the business belongs to your family, they are involved to one extent or another. In a family business, the members of your family become "partners," whether they take an active role in day-to-day operations or not. As a result, they need to be kept informed.

Discussing frustrations carried home from the job helps the family to understand your problems better. It also prevents them from getting the mistaken impression that they may have contributed to the problem in some way. Be careful, however, to see that your "discussion" of a problem does not turn into whining or, on the other end of the spectrum, an intemperate harangue or tirade. Often, in discussions of this sort, a member of the family may offer an excellent piece of advice on how to deal with the situation, or a solution to the problem will dramatically occur to you.

Round-table discussions of this sort provide valuable background and training for the members of the family who eventually may work in the business.

Let Off Some Steam, But Carefully

All of us have periods when it is necessary to let off steam. Consequently, most people can understand a brief flare-up when it occurs—as long as they have an awareness of the circumstances that caused it. Problems arise, however, when you get irritated at work and flare up at home, or become aggravated at home and flare up at work.

It's OK to blow your stack—let off some pressure—but *restrict it to the proper arena.* Don't make your family suffer because someone has messed up at work, or take it out on the employees because you have a problem at home.

The Family Is a Good Training Ground

It is the nature of business to be frenetic. People must be kept busy. Deadlines must be met. Competition must be countered. Old customers must be served, and new customers must be sought.

Life at home should be just the opposite. Tranquility should be the norm. Harmony ... rest and relaxation ... freedom from tension ... love and understanding...mutual support...a calm atmosphere—these should be the objectives at home.

- Keeping your commitments to the family can put you in the habit of meeting your commitments to customers.

- Practicing teamwork within the family can establish the skills that you will need for developing teamwork on the job.

- Delegating responsibilities around the home can give you the experience to delegate responsibility at work.

- Learning to be a consistent but fair disciplinarian at home can enable you to be consistent and fair when dealing with disciplinary matters on the job.

- Resolving problems within the family can teach you how to resolve personnel problems at work.

Problems at the Breakfast Table

Even in the happiest household, business-related arguments can arise, and all arguments within a family can be hurtful. Such arguments may involve situations that occur at home, but which are related to the office only in the most peripheral manner.

Some examples and some possible ways of dealing with them follow:

Problem: How to allocate money.   One wants to spend $20,000 on a new machine for the office; the other wants to spend the money to remodel the house.
Possible solution.   Business accounts and household accounts should be kept separately. It is a serious mistake to dip into company funds for household use and vice versa. Internal Revenue takes a dim view of it too.
Problem: How to balance your time between your work and your family.
Your wife wants to go to the movies, your son to a Little League game, your daughter to the shopping mall. And there's all that work at the office.
Possible solution.   Set a firm policy regarding the time you spend at work and live by it! That way, your family knows what to expect, your employees know what to expect, your customers know what to expect, and you know what to expect.

Emergencies and other unexpected "departures from the routine" will occur, and you *must* be flexible. But be sure that they are emergencies, and that you really are needed at work. Otherwise, stay with your schedule.

Problem: **Trying to explain which relative (or friend) you will hire and which one you won't, as well as how each employee (relative or not) is to be paid.**
Possible solution. Set a firm company policy regarding hiring, and another that establishes the pay scale. That way, your practices are clear and defensible.

If problems persist, delegate the hiring and firing, as well as the job of administering payroll, to another party—perhaps someone who is not a member of the family.

Further reflection may reveal that family disputes of this sort often are not at all what they seem. In fact, they may be an indication that your spouse or your children actually are voicing their resentment at the time (and possibly money) that you are devoting to your work. Ask yourself: "Am I becoming a workaholic? Should I be devoting more time and attention to my family?"

Your Home Isn't a Profit Center

Certainly, both a business and a home require a good budget. After all, outgo cannot exceed income. But the home isn't created to be a profit center, and it shouldn't be expected to function like one. Businesses are created to make money. Homes seldom if ever produce a profit.

Profit Can Take Many Forms

A number of years ago, I was talking to a farm implement dealer in northern California. He had immigrated to this country as a child and had had very little formal education, but his business was highly successful and I told him I'd like to see how he handled his record keeping. Proudly, he led me to the sales counter in his showroom.

"When we make a sale, the money goes in here," he said, pressing a key on the cash register. The cash drawer popped open, revealing neatly stacked rows of bills and coins representing the day's sales.

"When an invoice comes in, it goes here," he continued, reaching below the counter and extracting an old cigar box. Inside the cigar box I could see a couple of window envelopes, obviously bills that had arrived in the day's mail.

"And where is your spread sheet?" I asked. "The thing that shows you how much you're spending on rent, utilities, labor, parts, advertising, and all of that."

The dealer smiled, shrugged, and replied: "I don't have one."

"Well then, how do you know what profit you're making?" I asked.

"Young man," the old dealer replied quietly, "I came to this country when I was a little boy. All I had was what I wore—a shirt and a pair of pants. Today, I own this business; I have a nice home, and a little place in the mountains for the weekends. We own two cars and a truck, and we've raised two nice children—a boy and a girl, one a doctor and the other a lawyer. *The way I figure it, you add all of that up, deduct the shirt and the pants, and that's my profit.*"

The man's accounting procedures may have been a little primitive, but he certainly had learned the secret of keeping his life in perspective. He couldn't put a price on his pride, his home or his family, but after a lifetime of hard work, they were his "profit." Can any of us expect more?

Settle Differences Where They Happen

Avoid competition in the home. Leave that for work. Nevertheless, while the workplace and the home are two separate concerns, there is a great deal of overlap, particularly in family businesses. A family business "compresses" two worlds into one, adding an extra measure of strain to both.

If your son is also an employee, for example, any problems that originate in the home can carry over to the job and be reflected in his attitude and performance there. Similarly, any problems that originate on the job may carry over into his attitude and performance around home. For that reason, resolving problems as quickly as possible can be particularly important when a family business is involved. If some differences arise between you and your son at home, try to reach an understanding *before you go to work* and leave your differences behind. If those differences arise at work, *settle them there*; don't take them home.

If serious differences exist with a nonfamily employee at work, about the worst thing that can happen would be for the employee to quit. Serious differences at home can result in severe family problems ranging from rebellious children to runaways, from spousal spats to divorce.

If Necessary, Use an Arbitrator

Sometimes you will encounter a problem that would benefit from referral to some sort of arbitrator. Rather than allowing each individual to stubbornly maintain a position that is clearly unacceptable to the other, find a referee—a third party, such as your spouse—who can serve as a mediator and help you to resolve the problem in a way that will be agreeable to both sides.

This approach also can be used to solve many types of situations at work. There, just as at home, it often is possible to designate a neutral third party to help bring both sides of a dispute into accord.

Whether it's on the job or at home, showing someone "who's boss" is seldom as effective as reaching a mutually acceptable compromise.

A Word for the Workaholic

It requires a great deal of time and effort to start and maintain a successful business. Establishing and maintaining a family requires a great deal of time and effort too. In running a family business, the key is to find a suitable balance. When you spend too much time on the business, you become a workaholic and your family suffers. When you spend too much time with the family, the business generally suffers.

The best solution to this problem is to hire and train good personnel, then rely on those people to get the work done. Delegating responsibility to dependable employees is beneficial to the employees and it is beneficial to you. It tends to:

1. Give the employees self-confidence.
2. Boost their morale.
3. Provide them with an opportunity to develop and practice new skills.

Meanwhile, it affords you the opportunity to:

1. Concentrate on other important aspects of the business.
2. Relieve yourself of some of the tension that comes from running a business.
3. Afford the "luxury" of getting ill or taking a vacation.
4. Spend more time with your family.

Don't become a workaholic—a slave to your business. If you do, the business will suffer, you will suffer... and your family will suffer.

Business Is More Demanding

Running a business certainly calls for more rigidity than the average family can or would tolerate in the home.

At work, the boss's word may be law, and his or her instructions must be followed to the letter.

At work, you do as you are told or you stand the chance of losing your job. There is little room for someone who says, "I'll do it when I get around to it," or for someone who is careless with the company's money.

On the job, there must be constant pressure to see that all employees measure up to their expected levels of performance.

Not so in the home.

No Excuse for Laxity at Home

Obviously, this does not suggest that there isn't a need for authority in the family. Nor does it mean that children do not need discipline, should not be taught responsibility, or should not be encouraged to attain their fullest potential. At the same time, it is obvious that we can't act like the "family foreman" or treat our children as though they are part-time help.

> If some chore around the house is overlooked, it can probably be done the next day; but if an important customer's order goes unfilled, it might cost your company their business.

> If someone adds too much salt to the family dinner, you may have to eat out. But if someone at work puts too much of the wrong ingredient into a product—or puts the wrong part on a machine—the consequences might be far more serious. In some cases, law suits might even result.

> Your children may loll about all day on occasion, but if your employees loll about instead of doing their work, you could go bankrupt in a hurry.

No More Mr. Nice Guy

Being Mr. Nice Guy is what family life is all about, but running a business is not a popularity contest.

You are the one who must set the standards, lay out the rules, and see that the work gets done. These things are not negotiable, not debatable, not subject to a majority vote. And you are the one who is responsible for seeing that they are done. You must encourage teamwork, excellence, pride, and achievement.

Reward performance, but always try to be consistent, fair, and compassionate when doling out discipline. It is possible to be demanding without being blunt, overbearing, and tactless. Indeed, those are the worst characteristics to display in business because they can ruin your workers' morale, incentive and self-initiative.

One Rule Fits All

Both at home and at work, consistency is important. If a member of the family works in the business, it is important that he or she follow the same rules as any other employee, and suffer the same disciplinary action if a mistake is made. By treating a member of the family exactly as you would treat anyone else on the job, you show nonfamily employees that the rules are to be obeyed, no matter who is involved.

If you allow one company rule to be violated—no matter by whom— then all of the rules become suspect and your employees will begin to challenge one and then another in a test of wills. Soon you may find that you have lost control of the operation.

When the "Extended Family" Gets Involved

The potential for internal and intrafamily difficulty increases every time a business passes from one generation to the next. We will discuss both the problems of the extended family and the problems associated with succession in later chapters. It is fair to say, however, that these problems, like virtually all others, can be dealt with if the proper groundwork has been laid well in advance. The need for good communication, for consistency and fairness, for a means of arbitrating differences of opinion, and for having a clear separation between what happens on the job and what happens off the job can be particularly important.

Many family businesses involve relatives who do not live under the same roof, such as aunts and uncles, nieces and nephews, cousins, brothers and sisters, in-laws, or children who have grown up and established families of their own. In such situations, your authority may not be as absolute as it is when dealing with your spouse or with younger children. In fact, it may not be as absolute as it is when you are dealing with a total stranger.

Clear lines of authority and well-defined areas of responsibility are particularly important whenever the business involves relatives who do not live under the same roof. Petty family squabbles have destroyed many a good business.

How Tensions Develop

You can easily imagine the number of ways in which tension can multiply when (a) a parent joins the firm; (b) a number of the children join the firm, all working at different levels of responsibility; or (c) there are a number of outsiders in the firm, also working at different levels of responsibility.

As the head of the company, your loyalties are divided in many ways:

What does the family want you to do?

What do the outsiders want you to do?

What is best for the company?

Can you side with an outsider against a member of the family?

Should you support a member of the family (who, in this instance, may be wrong) against an outsider (who may be right)?

The dimensions of the debate are sufficiently drawn.

Family dynamics and business dynamics seldom mix. The objective is to draw the clearest possible distinction between the two and to make sure that everyone understands: The business is the business, and the family is the family. End of discussion.

Use Caution... and Set up Controls

A businessperson needs to be careful almost to the point of being suspicious. No detail can be overlooked, even temporarily.

Subtlety is often effective in the home, but in a business things generally tend to be more black and white, offering less room for gray areas. Gray areas tend to become too open to debate, to misinterpretation, to confusion, and therefore it is better to avoid them.

If there are two ways to do a job, both perfectly acceptable, it is better to state your preference and make that your standard than to have half of your people doing the job one way and half doing it the other.

When dealing with people, whether they are employees, customers, or suppliers, use *specific* words. Instead of "some," state a specific quantity. Instead of "maybe," say whether you will or won't.

Most helpful of all: Don't trust people's hearing or their memory. *Write things down!* See that everyone involved receives a copy. Set up a filing system that enables you to locate the document should you ever need it again.

Controls Can Help You Stay on Top of Things

Many businesses have failed for no other reason than the owner's failure to set down specific directions as to how things were to be done. Lacking such controls, each employee finds his or her own way to do things, quality control can be unheard of, inefficiency may run rampant, and waste can extend beyond belief. No wonder the businesses fail.

Lack of controls also contributes to workaholism. For want of suitable controls, it becomes necessary for the boss to be on hand every minute, making decisions and showing employees how their work is to be done.

If the business procedures were committed to paper, the work could go on in the boss's absence. Without such instructions, however, nobody knows what to do or how to do it when the boss is away. As a result, time off—even a vacation—becomes an impossibility.

Ensure Constant and Continuous Productivity

If you run short of materials, your production probably will fall behind. Employees may not be able to keep busy. Deliveries may falter. Sales may be lost. Customers may be lost. Competitors may move in. It may be necessary for you to pay higher prices in order to obtain urgent delivery of needed materials, thereby increasing your costs and reducing your profits.

Look at your production schedule. Determine how much raw material you need to have on hand. Institute an automatic system for reordering materials when your inventories run low.

Keep Your Work Force Active and Moving

If your employees are allowed to idle, it costs you money, which depletes profits. It also leads to a slump in their subsequent performance—a tendency to "roller coaster" between working hard and not working at all. It may lead to an indifferent attitude, not only toward the quantity of work they produce but toward its quality as well.

When employees feel that their management is sloppy, and when they have too much free time as well, they may turn to other activities such as:

Gossiping

Tying up the company telephones with personal calls

Playing pranks

Moonlighting on company time

Moonlighting with company resources

Taking extended rest and lunch breaks

...and so on

These types of activity tend to be contagious, resulting in more and more lost work hours. Once started, it can be extremely difficult to stop.

Unions usually are formed and thrive for two reasons (1) inept management and (2) underemployment—that is, not being occupied with productive work.

Watch your work force requirements carefully. Have enough people to handle the work, but be sure not to carry an excess of manpower "for the peak periods." It is better to bring in highly paid extra help than to engage the services of personnel who simply stand around and get in the way, even if they are less expensive.

If, at times, even your normal complement of personnel is more than you need to handle the day's work, *give them something meaningful to do*, such as cleaning and oiling the machinery, taking inventory, or attending a special training class.

Controls to Short-Circuit Employee Theft

Business losses due to employee theft have been increasing at an alarming rate. Money is not the only target. Raw materials, finished products, office supplies and machines, and even company secrets also are subject to theft when temptation—generally encouraged by loose controls—becomes too compelling. This sort of thing becomes contagious and difficult to stop.

On more than one occasion, I have heard of perfectly salable products being found on the trash heap, left there by a company employee. After hours, accomplices come by to pick up the merchandise, which they then convert to their own use and/or sell undercover.

Even the trash heap warrants careful scrutiny, and keeping a cautious eye on the company garbage dump can often be surprisingly revealing. A large amount of scrap can mean that there's too much waste, and hence a considerable amount of lost profit. A large quantity of discarded product can mean careless workmanship and highlight the need for better quality control.

Often, such behavior is felt to occur only among the lower-level employees. That is not true. Long-time, well-paid, highly respected employees in high-level positions have been known to walk away with a company's secrets—and its customer lists—in order to go into business for themselves. Behind them they leave the previous employer without a key executive, its most valuable business secrets, and many of its most important customers.

The most outlandish situations cannot be ruled out.

Learn to Welcome Outside Advice

As the leader of your family-run business, you set the goals for the benefit and welfare of your spouse and your children. Your goals become their goals for the most part, and helping you to achieve your goals enables them to achieve theirs. The family and the business, in such cases, are sometimes hard to separate. Yet, while I don't know of many people who would welcome outside advice as to how to run their families, those who refuse to get advice regarding the operation of their businesses take unnecessary risks.

Few businesses today function as they did in your parent's time. Many old-time family businesses have passed—or are rapidly disappearing:

- The mom and pop grocery store
- The community candy store
- The corner hardware store
- The independent druggist

The number of family-run farms is also declining.

Even the family doctor and lawyer have had to change their ways of doing business.

Keeping up with the Times

A wise businessperson realizes that changes occur daily—in new materials, improved design, more advanced technology, but also in such things as tax law, consumer trends, foreign and domestic competition, product liability, and labor relations. Responding to these factors quickly can insure greater profitability, a larger share of the market, and a viable business future. Failure to do so can result in product obsolescence, increased overhead, a decline in business, and even legal problems.

The task, then, is to find ways in which to obtain timely, reliable information about your business—in time to do something about it. The objective is not so much to find people who will tell you what you *must* do as it is to find people who can point out your various options. Once you have all of the necessary information and have weighed the pros and cons, the decision is up to you.

All of the following groups of people can provide valuable information and advice to anyone in any type of business:

Source	Type of information available
Bankers	How to arrange a loan How to set up a line of credit How to buy or sell abroad
Accountants	How to minimize your taxes How to set up your books How to get allowable tax breaks How to set your fees or prices
Lawyers	How to set up a corporation How to draw up a contract How to arrange a merger How to protect your company secrets How to enforce a contract How to defend against a lawsuit
Suppliers	How to buy most economically How to stay on top of the technology How to set the proper inventory levels How to buy in the most economical quantities
Customers	When prices are not competitive When quality is not satisfactory When service is substandard and/or noncompetitive
Employees	Where the inefficiencies are Who the best workers are Who the worst workers are Where to get new workers
Competitors	What direction the industry is going Trends in pricing Trends in new product or service development Trends in marketing New materials New methods of packaging New methods of distribution
Trade associations	Virtually everything attributed to customers and competitors above, plus what is going on in the international market and what trends may be working in government circles
Trade journals	In general, the same information that can be obtained from the trade associations
Consultants	In general, the same information that can be obtained from trade associations and trade journals, but with a more personal slant

Many companies spend a great deal of time and money to acquire this type of input. In addition to reading the trade publications and engaging consultants, as suggested above, they:

- *Conduct surveys,* in person or by mail, primarily among their most important customer groups, from whom they hope to learn new or better ways to get business.
- *Attend symposiums,* generally on very specific topics where they have a need for special expertise or experience.
- *Go to conventions,* where they can see the newest equipment, visit with their peers, listen to experts talking about special subject areas, make contact with potential suppliers, and so on.

... all in order to help them improve their businesses, increase their sales, reduce their overhead, and maximize their profit.

Profit Pointer

If you have a serious problem that involves experience outside of your own field of specialization (for the purpose of the example, let's say it's banking), you may get some good ideas by attending a banking seminar at the next annual meeting of your trade association.

But here's another suggestion: Either contact your bank or go directly to a representative of the American Banking Association to see if they will have a suitable seminar at their next convention. You may get a lot more information that way than you would from your own industry group.

When you have a medical problem, you go to a specialist. When you have a business problem, that's a good time to consult a specialist too.

(If your problem isn't banking, then find the association most directly related to the matter and approach it. Your local library can show you the Directory of Organizations and Associations, which lists all of the national and international trade associations.)

Sort the Good from the Not So Good

Admittedly, not all advice is *good* advice. Not all criticism is *constructive* criticism. But then it is also true that buried somewhere in that criticism and advice there is a hint—a trace ... a suggestion—that there is something that you might be doing better than you are now. If you can discover what that "something" may be—and act on it—you may be much better off for having made the effort.

_____ **FAMILY SUCCESS SCENARIO 13** _____

SPOTWISE PRODUCTIONS
Boston, Massachusetts

Larry Crowley almost learned the value of seeking and following outside advice too late.

Crowley headed a Boston-based company that produced educational and instructional films for industry. But in 1983, a stroke of good fortune resulted in a change in emphasis, and Spotwise Productions began to produce television commercials.

Income soared, but so did Crowley's business problems. In spite of increasing sales, the company was losing money. In effect, the company was headed toward bankruptcy.

Crowley was trained as a filmmaker and knew nothing about business management or finance—but he was determined to learn. He hired a consultant to work with him and to teach him the things he needed to know.

Although it was a slow and sobering experience, Crowley learned, bankruptcy was averted, and the company became a money maker, not a money loser ... because Crowley had the wisdom to heed his banker's advice.

Many other entrepreneurs have had the same sort of experience.

Making Company Goals and Employee Goals Mesh

The closer your goals are to those of your employees, the better the teamwork. The more successful you are in demonstrating to your employees that you *genuinely want to help them* reach their goals, the better their morale will be and the harder they will work. On the other hand, an employer who shows no regard for the employee or the employee's goals will surely have perpetual personnel problems, numerous disciplinary problems, poor productivity, and high turnover.

As your employees rely on you, so also do you—and your family—rely on them.

A Thought to Remember

At home, you take care of your children because you love them.
At work, you take care of your employees because you need them.

Give Yourself the People Advantage

How can you help your employees to achieve their goals while striving to attain your own? Put yourself in their shoes: What are their concerns?

1. *Earning a fair wage:* If your personnel are not receiving an attractive wage, they will not be happy with their work. This means that they will be sloppy, make mistakes, act in a surly fashion toward customers, do a lot of complaining, and take another job just as soon as they can find one that pays a higher wage.

2. *Other income-related benefits*:

- *Health insurance:* An important item these days, health insurance is most important to workers who have young children and to older workers, of course, but not to be ignored as an important consideration to all workers.
- *Life insurance:* Workers with young children are most concerned with life insurance. What will happen to my family, they ask, if something happens to me?
- *Child care services:* This topic is increasing concern as more and more women enter the work force. Whether they have a spouse or they are a single parent, what to do with the children during work hours is a major consideration.

3. *Job training:* Every line of work is becoming increasingly technical in nature. All workers realize, in their hearts, that they must continue to receive training if they are to have any hope of keeping their jobs, much less gain promotions.

Training employees is like making an investment in your future. The more you teach them to do, the more they have to contribute to your company.

4. *Specialized benefits*:

- *Savings plans:* These plans offer a way of encouraging your employees to save money. If they have some savings, they will be less dependent on continuous wage increases or various wage-related pressures from the unions, the job market, etc.

(Purely from the management point of view, you will suffer much less guilt if you have to lay off an employee whom you know has some savings tucked away than you will if that employee desperately needs a regular paycheck.)

- *Profit sharing:* Still one of the greatest incentives there is, profit sharing assures employees that their income relates directly to the profitability of the company. They're likely to work not only better, but smarter.

- *Retirement programs:* A good employee's reward for years of service should be a comfortable retirement. Your accountant, your banker, and your attorney can all give you some ideas about low-cost (even no-cost) retirement plans that your company could set up.

There often is the perception that these things are too costly and that a small business can't afford them. On the other hand, what does it cost to be perpetually advertising for, interviewing, and training new employees? What does it cost in spoilage if your personnel are not motivated? What is it worth to increase an employee's productivity by 10, 20, or 30 percent?

Perhaps it wouldn't be economical to set up a day care center for the employees in your company, but surely there are other companies that are the same size as yours and have a similar problem. Perhaps you can band them together and establish a *cooperative* center at an affordable cost.

Every problem has a solution—if you look for it.

Involving Employees in Goal Setting

Too often, people in business tend to keep their short- and long-range objectives to themselves—to treat them like family secrets. Generally, that is a faulty approach.

Can your family pack for a vacation when they don't know whether you're going to the mountains or the seashore? Can your secretary order an airline ticket without knowing whether you're headed for New York or Los Angeles? Can your employees put forth their best effort if they don't know what you are trying to achieve, how you are to achieve, and by when?

Take your employees into your confidence. Make them feel like insiders, like important members of your team. Tell them what you hope to do and show them precisely how they can help. Whenever possible, show the employees how they stand to benefit from helping you to reach your goals.

The result: *your* goals will become *their* goals, and your employees will work doubly hard to help you reach them.

Caring Can't Be Faked

Within the home, you probably set aside a little time every day to spend with each member of the family. The same tactic works wonders on the job.

_____ **FAMILY SUCCESS SCENARIO 14** _____

VAN BOEKHOVEN BOSCH
Utrecht, Holland

A friend of mine who had a printing company in Holland had a special way of dealing with people. He had several children, and each one was given a particular household chore to perform. The duty roster was posted on the refrigerator door, and on it were pasted bright gummed stars to acknowledge superior performance. His children competed vigorously to see who could earn the most stars.

Employees, he found, could be motivated in a similar manner. He made sure each employee knew his or her assignment and how he or she would be evaluated on it. He used visible things, such as a "business thermometer," to let everybody know how well they were doing. He incorporated various types of individual recognition—merit awards, certificates of merit, a special Employee of the Week parking spot—to stimulate a friendly spirit of competition between his employees.

Employee morale and performance increased tremendously.

Close ... but Not a Part of the Family

Such examples may suggest that you should run your business the same way you run your household, but that is not the point at all. Of course, there are some similarities between the home and the office, particularly in how you deal with people. But there also are a great many *differences* between how you should treat your employees and how you should treat the members of your family.

**Morale Booster: Changing and
Improving the Work Setting**

People spend almost as many hours each day in the place where they work as they do in their homes. Doesn't it stand to reason that a bright, clean, cheerful atmosphere is as important in the workplace as it is at home?

A friend of mine was being pestered by his wife to have the inside of their house repainted. Finally, he relented. The house got a fresh coat of paint and—lo and behold!—his spirits, his wife's spirits, and their children's spirits soared!

The following week, my friend looked around his place of business. The walls were drab, the windows were dingy, the drapes were threadbare, and the lighting fixtures were pockmarked with burned-out bulbs.

Was it his imagination, or were his employees going about their work in a listless, somber manner?

A few days later, my friend had the maintenance man replace all of the burned-out light bulbs. Painters redid the walls in a bright, cheerful color. New drapes were hung, and the windows were washed, inside and out. And lo!—the employees began to work harder and longer. They seemed to be more cheerful and get along better with each other. In addition, absenteeism dropped, production increased, and sales reached an all-time high.

Closeness is a hallmark of family life, but a businessperson can't afford to get too close to an employee. Too much familiarity can:

- Bring about a sense of intimacy that makes it difficult to maintain authority.
- Give other employees the impression that you are "playing favorites."
- Make it extremely difficult to administer disciplinary action or to give raises and make promotions.
- Make it difficult for middle managers to maintain control.

In still other situations, attempting to get too close to your employees can be interpreted by some to be "snooping," prying into their private lives. It can be perceived as encouraging one employee to spy on another.

Employees who speak as "buddies of the boss" become automatic contributors to the company gossip mill. Other employees get the impression that they're speaking for the boss, relating inside information that they have heard from the boss or reflecting the boss's attitude toward the condition of the business, employees' individual performances, and other intimate business details. That sort of gossip can undermine any organization.

Be friendly with your employees—caring, understanding, and compassionate—but always maintain your position of authority. That way, employees never feel that they have some special leverage with you, and you will never feel "indebted" to them.

A Thought to Remember

One of the primary differences between your family at home and your "family" at work is this: Your family at home encourages you to do the best that you can do. Your employees expect you to encourage them.

As the head of your family, you have its support; as the head of a business, you stand alone ... and are expected to provide support for the rest of the organization.

Chapter 3 Checkup

Questions for Jekyll and Hyde

Doctor Jekyll:

1. Who in your family would make a good arbitrator when it comes to a family dispute? Will you call on that person when the time comes?
2. List five things that you can to do to avoid becoming a workaholic.

(a) _____

(b) _____

(c) _____

(d) _____

(e) _____

3. Check each of those you have implemented in your own life so far.
4. If there are any that you have not checked, are you planning to put them into practice soon?

Mister Hyde:

1. Do you know the name and address of your trade association?
2. List the three things about which you are in the most desperate need for information right now.

    (a) _____

    (b) _____

    (c) _____

3. Write down where you plan to go for help in each of those three areas.

    (a) _____

    (b) _____

    (c) _____

4

Businesses Don't Run Themselves: They Need a Leader

Like a championship football team, a business needs a strong, capable leader. After all, a business doesn't run itself.

But what is this thing called leadership? The dictionary says: "Leadership—the quality of a leader: capacity to lead." Webster doesn't give us a clue as to what those qualities are, or what the "capacity to lead" amounts to. He doesn't even mention what kinds of people we are to lead. Presumably, a good leader can lead anyone.

If You've Got It, You've Got It

Some people obviously have leadership qualities and others do not. How can you tell a leader when you see one?

- Most people look pretty much the same.
- No birth certificate has "LEADER" stamped on it.
- You can't walk into a drugstore and buy a leadership pill.
- Leadership isn't something you can catch, like a virus.

- There are books about leadership, but I've never seen one that carries a money-back guarantee.
- Some colleges and universities offer courses in leadership, but every semester some will pass the course and others will fail.

It is not age or sex or the amount of money that one has, or is it the number of people who are involved. These are not the things that determine whether one is or is not a leader. Women can be leaders; men can be leaders. Boys and girls can be leaders. The elderly and the physically handicapped can be leaders. People can lead in little ways and in big ways. Some can lead many different activities at the same time.

Leaders Don't Just "Happen"—They Prepare

So what *is* leadership? What does it look like, where do you get it, and how can you tell if you've got it? Begging Mr. Webster's pardon, I submit that:

Leadership is a *skill*.

It's *voluntary*, meaning that you must take it upon yourself.

And it's *developed through practice*.

The day you step forward and say "I'll do it" is the day you become a leader. The more often you do that, and the greater the number of people who elect to follow you in whatever you have volunteered to do, the more skillful a leader you become.

Use It or Lose It

Leadership is an *active* thing. You are a leader only as long as you continue to lead. If you stop leading, you no longer are a leader.

Now what about those "qualities of a leader" that Mr. Webster wrote about?

How to Lead a Family Business

Family business leaders are self-confident and assured.   They should know what must be done most of the time or be able to find out the best course. They also should feel that they know how to get it done, if not by themselves then with the help of others. This self-confidence inspires other people to follow. If the leader's self-confidence falters, the others will sense it and falter too. Leaders must never let that happen; they must continue to lead.

False bravado, braggadocio, and bossiness are not acceptable ways of demonstrating one's self-confidence. A leader's power stems from the fact that he or she has been able to gain the respect of associates. Braggarts and loudmouths seldom win respect.

Leaders are decisive.   Because they know what has to be done and how to do it, they can show others what to do. They can keep people headed in the right direction, and prevent them from taking detours, going down blind alleys, aimlessly wandering about.

If there are forks in the road, they select the right path. If the road contains obstacles, they find a way to remove them. With intense concentration, they keep the project moving forward—always headed toward their objective.

Leaders know how to delegate.   Realizing that they can't do everything themselves, and that others cannot accomplish much unless they have enough authority to do their work, the leader delegates authority to the staff—no more authority than is necessary, to be sure, but certainly no less.

Because they are confident and self-assured, leaders do not feel threatened when they delegate authority. On the contrary, they realize that their power stems from what is accomplished, so they are eager to do whatever they can to help subordinates accomplish as much as possible.

Leaders don't always carry the ball themselves, but they designate who will.

Leaders know how to motivate.   To get the most out of people, they must be motivated. They must *want* to do their work, and the incentive of a paycheck often is not strong enough to bring out a worker's best efforts.

A good leader knows how to make the work sound like fun—how to flatter a worker into believing that nobody else could do the job quite as well and that, paycheck aside, the rewards of a job well done are within reach.

Family business leaders know the value of teamwork.   They know that two people can accomplish more than one, and that three can accomplish more than two. They know that Superman does not exist, and so they form teams of people who possess the right combinations of skills to get the job done.

At the same time, they know that a team needs direction, a reasonable timetable, the necessary resources and suitable authority. So they provide it with those things.

Leaders monitor progress.   Having assigned the work, delegated the authority, and provided the necessary people, equipment, material, and funds to get the job done, leaders make it a point not to interfere. They may step in to help out in a crisis, *but they let their people do their work.*

Point Them in the Right Direction

Maintaining just enough control to see that the work gets done—and gets done properly—effective family business leaders concentrate on their own unique duties. To provide leadership, they must:

■ Survey the total picture.
■ Evaluate short- and long-term objectives.
■ Study the market.
■ Monitor the competition.
■ Accurately assess their own company's situation.

That is the only way to keep the organization headed in the right direction.

Why the Boss's Job Is "Different"

The process of operating a business is not as easy and straightforward as it may seem.

Let's study an example by simplifying the operation of a McDonald's fast food restaurant. According to recent figures, one out of 15 of today's young adults got his or her first job in a McDonald's.

The Purpose Is to Make Money, Not Hamburgers

McDonald's makes and sells hamburgers. Therefore, it would seem likely that operating a McDonald's franchise simply calls for someone who can cook a hamburger, hand it to the customer, take the money, and put the money in the cash register. Obviously, there is more to it than that—possibly a great deal more than you ever would have imagined.

Cooks Cook, Managers Manage

The process begins long before the first hamburger is cooked and served.

Somebody surveys the community to find a vacant piece of property (a) large enough to build on and (b) in a location where there will be a good deal of traffic. The property must then be purchased or leased, which probably will require going to a bank to arrange for financing.

A bank will not lend money to someone who does not have a fully detailed business plan showing where the owner expects to get enough money to repay the loan. Someone has to prepare such a business plan.

Once the loan is acquired, the property can be bought (or leased).

Then the building has to be erected.

How large should it be?

How long should the counter be?

How many seats should the restaurant have?

How many cash registers, soft drink dispensers, food trays, straws, napkins, and plastic cups will be needed?

How large should the refrigerator be?

What other kitchen equipment will be required?

How large should the parking lot be?

What color should the walls be painted?

Does your proposed sign conform to local ordinance requirements?

Now you will need to arrange for a building inspection and get a restaurant license.

You will have to hire and train your personnel.

You will have to order your food and supplies. Not enough food and you lose sales; too much and it will spoil or go stale.

As long as you stay in business, the cycle goes on. Fresh food must be ordered regularly. People leave and must be replaced. Equipment malfunctions must be repaired. If vandals break a window, it has to be replaced and reported to the insurance company. The payroll, the suppliers, the utilities, the mortgage, and the income taxes have to be paid. Paperwork has to be completed.

The easiest part of the job is cooking and selling the hamburgers. Hired help can do that. The owner has too much else to do.

Lead and Supervise

Some businesses are less complex than running a fast food restaurant. Many, however, are far more complex. The leader must demonstrate the self-confidence and decisiveness to maintain authority, be able to delegate responsibility and rely on teamwork, and provide the supervision needed to keep things running smoothly.

McDonald's provides an excellent example for lessons related to business because the company has become one of the great success stories of modern times. It was a pioneer in fast food, in franchising, in employee training, and in setting and maintaining high operating standards.

A similar, though less well-known success story involves Al Copeland, founder of Popeye's.

_____ **FAMILY SUCCESS SCENARIO 15** _____

POPEYE'S FAMOUS FRIED CHICKEN & BISCUITS
New Orleans, Louisiana

Al Copeland grew up in a housing project and dropped out of high school at the age of 16. During the day, he worked at a supermarket soda counter; at night, in his brother's doughnut shop.

By the time he was 18, Copeland had managed to save enough money to buy his own doughnut shop, but he wanted something more.

New Orleans is in the heart of America's Cajun country, where hot pepper-laden food is a tradition. So in 1972, Copeland opened Chicken on the Run, a restaurant featuring chicken prepared according to a toned-down Cajun recipe. He lost almost $13,000 during his first year.

Copeland spiced up his chicken recipe and renamed his restaurant Popeye's. By 1988, Popeye's was the third largest chicken chain in the country with 725 outlets and $500 million in sales.

Copeland owns 96 percent of Popeye's, has a personal fortune estimated at over $200 million, lives in a 26-room New Orleans mansion, and operates his company out of a fifth-floor office in Popeye Plaza. He has branched out with a series of up-scale Copeland's Cajun-American Cafes, and he has acquired Church's Fried Chicken, the second largest chicken chain in the country (with 1,500 outlets, nearly twice the size of Popeye's, although both chains are approximately equal in sales volume).

Learn How to Work Smart

What is it that enables a Ray Kroc (McDonald's) or an Al Copeland (Popeye's) to attain such phenomenal success? Obviously, they are leaders, but they have been so remarkably successful that they have attained a super-star status.

The answer is: both men have learned to "work smart." If McDonald's Ray Kroc did not spend his time cooking hamburgers, what was he doing? Highly successful people, various studies have shown, reach exceptional levels of performance by learning how to manage their resources extremely well. Others work with the same resources — time, money, and manpower — but the super-successful have been able to do more with what they have than most others.

In a recent book, *Real Managers*, the authors discovered that highly successful leaders spend just 13 percent of their time handling traditional management functions and only 11 percent of their time managing their human resources. Over one-fourth of their time is spent on routine communications and nearly 50 percent of their time is spent "networking" — maintaining liaison with people *outside the company* who can help them develop a better, stronger, more efficient business.

Networking is one of the most popular buzz words in business today, and we will explore it more fully later in this chapter.

Learn to Use the Tools

To accomplish more within the normal work day, successful leaders have learned to manage their time more effectively.

They have adopted telephones, computers, facsimiles, photocopiers, and other machines to relieve them of some of their workload.

They have learned to avoid procrastination.

They have learned to prioritize their work, doing the most important jobs first.

They have learned to set up *tomorrow's* agenda *today* so that they will know exactly what they will be doing as soon as they reach the office in the morning.

They have learned to set realistic deadlines — and meet them.

In *Rate Your Executive Potential* — a book I did fairly recently — an entire section is devoted to the subject of time management, for example:

How to tell if you're using your time wisely

Learning to appreciate what your time is worth

Tips on how to manage your time more efficiently, and how to avoid wasting time

How to set up and maintain a daily time log

Saving time on the telephone, and at meetings

I won't go into those things in detail here, except to point out that *the key to success does not mean working longer hours*; it means *working smarter*.

Workaholics Aren't Productive

Thomas Horton, who now heads the American Management Association, discovered this principle when he was an executive with IBM. Striving for success, Horton began to work 14-hour days and seven-day weeks. He found himself growing stale and his work became less and less effective. Horton broke out of his workaholic rut, began to devote more time to himself and his family, and found that it made him more productive both on and off the job.

Overhead: Is It an Expense or an Investment?

To manage money resources more wisely, executives must learn exactly *where* their money comes from and exactly *where it is going*. They must set a profit objective: 10 percent, 20 percent, 30 percent. Then they must take the steps necessary to attain that objective.

Too many executives, for example, look at the monthly payroll and view the figure they see there as their cost of labor. They fail to realize that their true cost of labor is probably several times that amount due to taxes, fringe benefits, space requirements, equipment requirements, support services, and other costs should be added in.

Too many executives look at their overhead as an expense, and not as an investment. If you begin to think of your expenses as an investment, you can begin to answer such questions as:

Is this operation producing a sufficient return for what it's costing me? (If the answer is no, then some decisions have to be made.)

Is the operation necessary in the first place?

What *is* the function worth?

Can the job be done for less cost?

Can the work be done differently, somewhere else in the company, or by an outside source?

Once you have a good idea of what each operation is worth to the company, as well as clear, accurate and up-to-date information as to its cost, you can act, rather than react to ever changing business situations.

People Are an Investment Too

When you manage time and money, you are dealing with impersonal items. Not so when you are dealing with the most important—and probably the most costly—of your resources: people. People are an investment too. You hire then, train them, equip them, pay them a salary, and expect them to contribute to the profitability of the firm.

Proper training involves a number of things. It is not simply how to operate a machine, how to write up an order, or how to fill out government forms that matters; it's also showing them where they fit into the organization, why they are important to the organization, what the organization's true objectives are, and how *they* can prosper if *the company* prospers.

FAMILY SUCCESS SCENARIO 16

PERMA-DOOR
Cincinnati, Ohio

To Dennis Vehr, the objective of his company, Perma-Door, is not to *make* ornamental steel doors, but to *sell* ornamental steel doors *at a profit*. Toward that end, Vehr makes an effort to convince every employee that, in one fashion or another, they are all Perma-Door salespersons.

When Perma-Door customers take a tour of the plant, their guide is not an executive, but one of the company's 100 line workers. That way, says Vehr, the employees interface, like salespeople, with the company's customers, which gives them an opportunity to demonstrate their pride in their work.

The customers, in turn, not only learn more about Perma-Door's product, but they have an opportunity to get to know the people who actually make it.

Job Training: A National Priority

With the rapid changes in technology that have been occurring since World War II, the need for constant training and retraining has never been more important. Yet American business, on the whole, is doing a very poor job in that area. In the United States, only one-tenth of one percent of our gross national product is invested in job training. By contrast, Japan spends 10 percent of its GNP on training.

David Packard, chairman of Hewlett-Packard, thinks that "focus" is an important part of job training. He feels that a company's employees should be directed to concentrate on only one or two key goals at a time. In that manner, their efforts are centered on a common objective rather than to many other activities that may be more interesting, more challenging or more fun, but of less importance to the company.

Motivation: Another Priority

Regardless of their specific job assignments, employees need constant motivation. The promise of a regular paycheck is not enough. They also need to feel good about what they are doing; know that they are making a significant contribution, not only to the company but to the community, if possible; and most of all, know that their efforts are appreciated.

Many employers tend to confuse a happy employee with a well-motivated employee. That may not be so. A happy employee is not necessarily productive, therefore he is not necessarily well motivated. A *productive* employee is well motivated, whether or not he is "happy."

Any effort toward employee motivation must result in an upturn in productivity, efficiency, profitability. Improved morale, which generally follows, is a plus. Poor motivation will cause an individual to do something that will please *you*; but good motivation will cause people to do things that will please *themselves*.

Delegation Contributes to Motivation

One means of stimulating motivation is to delegate responsibility to your employees. It signifies that you have confidence in them and respect their abilities.

Proper delegation is a multistep process:

1. *You must clearly define the objective.*

"We want you to do a better job" is not specific enough.

"We'd like you to turn out 100 invoices an hour" is much better.

2. *You must put priority on things.*

"We need to clean up this place" might encourage an employee to drop everything and reach for the broom.

"After you're finished with that job, we'd like for you to clean up around your work area" tells the employee that his work comes first and that the clean-up can follow.

3. *You must be sure that the employee knows how to do the job.*

Although you have previously gone over the procedure several times, ask the employee to tell you how she plans to do the job that you have delegated to her. She will be proud to demonstrate what she has learned, and at the same time, you will have an opportunity to see that she will do it right, or correct her if she plans to do it wrong.

4. *You must provide the employee with adequate resources to do the job.*

Assign a team of people to work with him. Instruct other departments to give him their support. Provide him with an adequate budget. Don't assign him to a task that has failure already built into it.

5. *You must be sure to preserve company policy and protocol.*

To tell an employee that you would like him to handle the Consolidated Cornfield matter tends to imply a measure of carte blanche. To add "be sure to clear everything through Legal" reminds him that he must abide by established procedures.

6. *You must maintain some degree of supervision.*

Telling someone to "take care of the Amalgamated Apple situation" can be improved tremendously by adding, "Come in next Thursday and tell me how you're doing."

Delegating responsibility to other people is not easy for many people to learn even when those people are members of their own family. Some fear that they will be less important if they don't do everything themselves. Some fear that a subordinate will take the delegated authority and use it against them. Others, usually in middle management positions, fear that they may be creating a competitor for future promotions. Sometimes a failure to delegate is caused by nothing more than sibling rivalry.

All of these are faulty assumptions, and all are based on fear (another term for "lack of self-confidence," which must never be the case in a true leader).

Countless excuses are given for failing to delegate:

- *"Jo isn't ready to handle that job."*

If that's true, you haven't given Jo the proper training. Often, you'll never know if an employee is ready unless you give her a chance.

- *"I can do it faster myself than it will take me to explain the job to Andrea."*

  But once having explained it to Andrea, she'll be able to do it again and again. That's what training is all about. And you'll have more time to do other things.

- *"I can do the job better than Kelly."*

  Again, that's only because Kelly hasn't been properly trained. Besides, Kelly may have a different perspective on the job and may be able to devise a way of doing it even better. Give her a chance.

These are not really reasons for Jo (or Andrea or Kelly) not being able to do the job. They are excuses for your not assigning the job to them. Be honest with yourself and be fair to your employees.

No team will hit a home run every time at bat and no two successes are equally valuable. Success is relative. A 5-percent gain in one area may be more significant than a 20-percent gain in another.

You Can't Do It Once and Then Forget It

Groups of people tend to go through periods of letdown, making it difficult to perform at peak level all of the time. An astute leader should be able to regenerate employees' motivation so that they can move on to another objective.

1. *Instead of dwelling on your past success, excite your employees about the challenges ahead.*

After they have had their pat on the back, the employees need to have their energies directed toward their next assignment.

2. *Don't give the project leader all the credit.*

Let everyone know that they contributed to the success and that their efforts were seen and appreciated. Be as specific as possible in praising each participant.

3. *Delegate the next task to a different employee.*

The one who headed the last effort will have a chance to savor his success and regroup, while the new leader will be fresh, fired up, and eager to show you what he can do.

4. *Try to find a new approach, rather than attempting to imitate what you did the last time.*

This will be more exciting and challenging for the employees, and it will discourage your competitors from creating a counterstrategy.

5. *Develop new skills among your employees.*

If your last success was in the retail field, try going after the institutional market. If it was in selling hamburgers, try introducing a fish sandwich. If it was in newspaper advertising, try spot TV.

It has been said that management's five biggest mistakes are:

1. Being overconfident
2. Rationalizing bad decisions
3. Placing too much trust in the first piece of information at hand
4. Seeking only the kind of evidence that will support your point of view
5. Relying on only one source of information.

All of these point to the need for seeking and heeding outside advice.

Supplementing and Complementing Talents

Because of such human frailties, many modern companies are shunning sole proprietorships and moving toward partnerships among people who have knowledge of management, people who know finance, and people who can handle sales. They learn to seek the advice of employees and customers as well.

When James Jewett, founder of Telco Research Corporation, was asked to develop a $50,000 product for Ingersoll Rand, for example, he was reluctant. Would it be worth Telco's energies to develop such a product for only one client? Hearing this, Ingersoll Rand found five other companies that were interested in the same product, and Jewett was convinced. Telco developed the product ... at a nice profit ... and in 1986, sold out to another company for 50 times earnings.

In this case, Telco received outside help from one of its customers. Other possible sources of assistance are:

U.S. Small Business Administration

Business schools and colleges

American Woman's Economic Development Corp. (AWED)

Women's Business Development Center

Service Corps of Retired Executives (SCORE)

U.S. Office of Women's Business Ownership

American Business Women's Association

National Association of Women Business Owners

... and many, many more

Networking Can Work ... But It's No Cure-All

These days, the mixing and mingling of people, each trying to make business connections outside their own companies, is called "networking." It can be done in person, by phone or by mail. In the past, it was known as "having the right connections" or "knowing the right people" and stemmed from the old adage: "It's not *what* you know, but *who* you know." Cynical, perhaps, but often true.

The wonderful thing about networking is that it is a matter of one person seeking another for the mutual benefit of both. Everyone wins; nobody loses.

Jerry Rubin, a Yippie who was one of the infamous Chicago Seven during the 1968 Democratic National Convention, is said to have taken networking to the level of a fine art. His formula: attend a function, make 20 contacts, and set up two lunches.

As popular as it may be, networking is not a cure-all, however. Meeting the right kind of contact in this manner can be pure hit and miss, and sometimes a businessperson can't wait until the right connection comes along. In addition, there's no guarantee of equality through networking. You may help other individuals far more than they are able to help you. Generally, the smaller, the more technical, the more limited a business is, the less likely it will be to stumble across an ally through networking.

A more direct approach is to seek help from a lawyer, a banker, or possibly a consultant. There are consultants who specialize in virtually every phase of business. For example, Peter Williams, founder of Aspen Ribbons of Lafayette, Colorado was losing money because of inefficient packaging. Williams hired a consultant who saved his company $100,000 a year. The cost: $5,000.

Whether dealing with time, money, or people — consulting with your lawyer, reading the trade publications, or engaging a consultant — it is important to remember, at all times, that *you are the leader*.

Businesses do not run themselves. *You* took the job. *You* must take control, make the decisions, set the course, and guide your company to success.

Chapter 4 Checkup

Rate Yourself as a Leader

1. Evaluate your skills in key areas of leadership according to a scale of 1 to 10.

	Low									High
Self-confidence	1	2	3	4	5	6	7	8	9	10
Decisiveness	1	2	3	4	5	6	7	8	9	10
Ability to delegate authority	1	2	3	4	5	6	7	8	9	10
Ability to offer motivation	1	2	3	4	5	6	7	8	9	10
Encourage teamwork	1	2	3	4	5	6	7	8	9	10
Faithfully monitor progress	1	2	3	4	5	6	7	8	9	10

2. Duplicate this quiz and ask each member of your family to evaluate your skills as *they* see them — anonymously, of course.

3. Duplicate the quiz and ask each *nonfamily* member of your company evaluate your skills as they perceive them — once again, with the assurance of anonymity.

Compare your family's answers to your own. Also compare the answers of the nonfamily workers, not only to your own answers but to those that were given by members of your family.

If you scored a 7 or less in any area, you probably should consider working to bolster your skills in that area.

5
Spouses: Lovers and Partners

Whatever the short- and long-term socioeconomic implications may be, one fact of modern life is undeniable: The "traditional" American household is rapidly disappearing, perhaps never to return. In its place, there are the DINKs and the DEWKs. A DINK family has Dual Income, No Kids. A DEWK family has Dual Employment *With* Kids.

With or without the children, a modern family usually includes *two* employed adults. In some cases, those adults work together; in others, they work for separate employers. Either way, the difficulties involved when both adults work tends to impose additional stress around the home.

Redividing the Responsibilities

No longer is the care of the home the nearly exclusive realm of the female partner. Now a division of those duties—housecleaning, cooking, dishwashing, laundry—is required.

There is the question of "his" money versus "her" money, and most often, both go into a common fund. But occasionally there are economic differences when it comes to buying a luxury item that one partner wants and the other does not.

Vacations even become more complicated. It often is not easy for both partners to get away from work at the same time—particularly if they are managing a growing business together.

What About the Kids?

Parenthood takes on added complexity that ranges from scheduling a convenient time for child-bearing to determining who will look after the offspring once born.

Day care centers have done a lot to relieve some of the child-related tensions in young families, but they certainly do not solve all of the problems—and they even impose an additional burden when it comes to the family budget.

When both spouses have a job, there is at least twice the job-related tension, which all too often carries over into the home. When the two jobs come into conflict, which one will receive the preference?

How About the Possibility of Relocation?

The most distressing situation may occur when a company wishes to relocate one of its employees.

What about the spouse? And the spouse's job?

Can the spouse find comparable employment at the new location?

Is it practical for the spouse to give up a good job (possibly a promotion), fringe benefits, and retirement plan in order to join his or her partner in a move?

Do you go or stay?

What is best?

If one spouse is as outstanding an employee as the other, the two employers might end up in a tug of war over the situation. A "salary war" could result. Relations between the two companies could be damaged. A third company could intervene, and walk off with both spouses.

To keep the desired employee, and move the family unit to a new location without seriously damaging its income, some companies actually have been compelled to find (or create) some kind of job for the spouse at the point of relocation.

Sometimes the Answer Is a Business of Your Own

Increasingly, problems of this sort are being resolved by husbands and wives who decide to go into business together. No more "his" job versus "her" job. No more problem with scheduling time off that might be convenient to both employers. No more questions about which is more important: your spouse or your job.

_____ FAMILY SUCCESS SCENARIO 17 _____

T. J. CINNAMON'S
Kansas City, Missouri

In 1982, Ted and Joyce Rice began to find life closing in on them. Ted had worked as a news cameraman at a Kansas City television station for 18 years; Joyce was a teacher.

Ted often worked nights, and Joyce worked days. They had little time together, and their children were getting older. So, in 1982, the Rices took a four-month leave to sail Lake Superior with their son Sam. That's when they decided to start a business of their own.

Two years later, Joyce and her sister started hauling a 20-foot trailer to state fairs and rodeos throughout the south and the midwest in order to test market some cinnamon rolls that Joyce had prepared. Consumer response was excellent.

A few months later, Ted took early retirement from the television station, and the following January (1985), the Rices opened the first permanent T. J. Cinnamon's bakery in a Kansas City shopping center.

The next spring, Ken Hill, the president of Gilbert/Robinson Inc., a restaurant division of W. R. Grace & Co., visited the Rices with an unusual offer.

Hill would quit Gilbert/Robinson and join T. J. Cinnamon's as its president, specializing in franchises. Ted Rice would become chairman of the reorganized firm; Joyce, vice president in charge of training.

During the ensuing six months, T. J. Cinnamon's sold 140 franchises, and became a national byword!

The Number of New Family Businesses Is Up

The U.S. Small Business Administration points out that the number of joint proprietorships—a business structure favored by many couples going into business—increased by over 20 percent between 1980 and 1986.

William and Virginia Van Hee of Rochester, New York are one couple that entered business as a husband and wife team. They started their heating and air conditioning company, using one corner of their house as an office where Ginny could keep the books. Bill used the family station wagon to transport his tools and equipment.

Now, Bill is president and treasurer of the firm, Ginny is vice president and secretary, and the company has 11 employees.

Another enterprising couple, Martha and David Kimmel, formed Mommy Made, a fresh baby food company in New York City on an investment of $50,000 in 1987. Within a year, they were supplying 150 customers throughout Manhattan; and they now hope to go nationwide. Their goal: $25 million in sales by 1993.

The Opportunities Exist

The opportunities are there for those who are willing to take the chances and do the hard work that is necessary to get a business going. The Center for Entrepreneurial Management in New York estimates that some 40 percent of America's gross national product is generated by family firms.

_____ FAMILY SUCCESS SCENARIO 18 _____

SUNRISE RETIREMENT HOMES, INC.
Arlington, Virginia

Terry and Paul Klaasen were living in Arlington, Virginia when they learned that an abandoned nursing home nearby was for sale. The asking price was $500,000; the Klaasens offered $300,000.

To raise the $75,000 down payment, the Klaasens sold their townhouse and borrowed some money from friends.

The couple lived with family for three months while they fixed up the nursing home. After that, Terry quit her job as a pension benefits expert to find customers for their new business. Paul continued to work part time as the administrator of a taxpayers' lobby at the U.S. Chamber of Commerce.

The purchase of the nursing home closed in December. Two days later, the first two people moved into the nursing home. Seven months after that, there were 14 residents, and the business broke even.

Now there are more than 80 residents at the original home, and Sunrise Retirement Homes, Inc. has opened two more facilities. The Klaasens are now franchising their business, and have purchased a child care center for diversification.

Family Businesses: The New Revolution

This trend has been characterized as something of a modern revolution. Over 18 million Americans worked out of their homes in mid-1987, according to the U.S. Department of Labor, although that total probably is understated because most part-time and unlicensed "cottage industries" are not included in the government's figures.

Home-Office Computing Magazine conducts an annual survey among those who operate a home-based business. The latest figures indicate that those who operate such businesses are people who:

- Average 40 years of age.
- Are married (75 percent).
- Have children (70 percent).
- Are male (62 percent) and female (38 percent).
- Have worked at home less than 10 years.

Of particular interest is the fact that 98 percent of the magazine's respondents said that *they are happier* working at home, and 97 percent said they definitely *would recommend* working at home!

FAMILY SUCCESS SCENARIO 19

BLUE MOUNTAIN ARTS
Culver City, California

Susan and Stephen Polis gave up the rat race in 1971 and turned to something that they truly love: poetry and art.

The Polis's formed Blue Mountain Arts and began to create all occasion greeting cards featuring Susan's poetry.

To date, over 200 million cards have been sold, and Blue Mountain has become a company of 100 employees.

Does a Family Business Lead to Liberation or Confinement?

There are a great many personal freedoms to be enjoyed by having a business of your own. At the same time, there is no "big brother" to hand you a weekly paycheck so you can meet your financial obligations.

Some people find their own business to be a symbol of freedom; others find it to be quite the opposite.

_____ **FAMILY SUCCESS SCENARIO 20** _____

3-D PHOTOGRAPHY
Culver City, California

In 1978, Susan Pinsky and her husband David Starkman parlayed their interest in 3-D photography into a profitable business.

Turning a small bedroom into an office, Susan and David started to distribute a newsletter about 3-D. After that, they began to manufacture a few hard-to-get photo accessories, and soon the business outgrew their Duarte, California home, so they moved to Culver City.

The couple now produces an illustrated 24-page catalog that features several hundred products, books, viewers, and camera accessories, and they mail it to 9,000 customers.

"We work all of the time," says Susan, "but there's no commute. We don't have to be dressed up. We don't waste time on the freeways or going out to lunch."

What's the Attraction?

Having no dress code and being able to avoid commuter delays are some of the benefits of having your own business. There also are many other things that you may be able to leave behind if you strike out on your own.

Robert Half, a San Francisco-based recruiting firm, conducted a survey to see why people leave one job and move on to another. The findings:

47 percent	Quit because their jobs offered limited opportunities for advancement.
26 percent	Quit for lck of recognition.
15 percent	Quit because they were unhappy with management.
6 percent	Quit because of inadequate salary or benefits.
6 percent	Quit because they were bored with their work

_____ **FAMILY SUCCESS SCENARIO 21** _____

FOREIGN CANDY CO.
Hull, Iowa

In the early 1970s, the De Yager family found its opportunity in Europe. That year, Peter De Yager took his high school German class to Europe, and there his students came across a particularly delightful candy.

Returning home, Peter and his wife Betsy decided to set up an office in their basement, import the European candies, and sell them through a network of midwestern high school language teachers.

The Gummy Bear caught on, then the Gummy Worm, and ultimately a series of other gummy goodies.

In 1978, the De Yagers formed the Foreign Candy Co., which today is a $9 million import business, operating nationwide with 45 full-time employees.

People Make Moves for a Variety of Reasons

The previously mentioned survey by *Home-Office Computing Magazine* also asked why people had given up their "regular" job and gone into a home-based business. The main reasons given:

51 percent	I wanted to be my own boss.
42 percent	I wanted to make more money.
31 percent	I wanted to change my life.
30 percent	I wanted to spend more time with my family.
27 percent	I'm more productive at home.
21 percent	I'd gone as far as I could in the corporation.
19 percent	I hated the commute.

_____ **FAMILY SUCCESS SCENARIO 22** _____

TICA DEVELOPMENT CORP.
Westchester, New York

Sal Americo was working as an architect in Manhattan. His wife Kathy was a former administrator in a nursing home. Desiring a better life, they had invested in several rental houses together.

Then, in 1980, the Americos moved from Manhattan to Westchester. That is when they decided to form Tica Development Corp., a real estate development company.

The Americos found a site in Ossining that overlooks the Hudson River. By taking out second mortgages on their rental properties, they acquired $130,000, which they used on engineers' reports, on getting approvals from the city planning board, and on options to buy 11 acres of land. Sal drew up plans for the construction of 82 townhouses.

Then came the bad news: Bankers would not lend the Americos any more money with which to go ahead.

In February 1985, at a family get-together in honor of their daughter's baptism, ten friends and relatives surprised the Americos by pledging $400,000 to their townhouse project.

With that money, Sal and Kathy exercised their options and purchased the land that they needed. Using the land as collateral, the Americos then were able to arrange a $550,000 bank loan and to borrow $150,000 to get utilities to the property and make other site improvements.

Construction financing increased the Americos' indebtedness to $2.2 million, but their project was underway.

Sal quit his job in Manhattan to become the general contractor, while Kathy ran the company and supervised their three salespeople. By the first quarter of 1989, all 82 of their townhouses had been sold.

A Steady Paycheck: Insurance During Startup

Startups are always difficult, and even entrepreneurs need to eat and pay their bills.

When Alan Cottrill and his wife opened their first pizzeria in Washington, Pennsylvania in 1981, they had to live in the back of the restaurant with their young son. Today, the Cottrills operate 90 restaurants and have an annual income of over $30 million.

The spouse's role as the family provider during the early days of a new business startup has been retold many times. An excellent example involves Craig Mascolo, who lived on his wife's small salary, supplemented by unemployment checks, for six months while he struggled to get a heavy construction company started.

Far from being uncommon, the spouse's paycheck keeps the family afloat during the early stages of starting a business in one case out of every five according to a recent study conducted by a prominent national business magazine.

_____ FAMILY SUCCESS SCENARIO 23 _____

THE CAR BOOK
Washington, D.C.

Jack Gillis worked for the U.S. Department of Transportation, where he produced a publication called *The Car Book*, a consumer information guide that reached two million people a year. It was the most popular government publication in history.

The Car Book was discontinued, however, in a drive to reduce government spending during the Reagan administration. Gillis quit his job and decided to publish the guide himself.

While the Gillis family lived off the income of Jack's wife, his mother invested her life's savings in his project.

For a year, Gillis sold his book door to door. Then publisher E. P. Dutton agreed to produce a hardcover version of the book, and in 1986, Harper & Row publishing company gave Gillis a six-figure advance for the right to print the book in a paperback version.

If at First You Don't Succeed...

Not every business venture meets with immediate success. Some entrepreneurs have had to try again and again before they could get a successful family business off the ground.

_____ FAMILY SUCCESS SCENARIO 24 _____

BLANCHARD & BLANCHARD & SON LTD.
Norwich, Vermont

Robert Blanchard was a social worker in St. Johnsbury, Vermont, and his wife Melinda worked for Planned Parenthood. Both were discouraged with their work. In 1975, their house burned down.

Using their $8,000 insurance settlement, the couple started Board & Basket, a retail store featuring cookware and tabletop items, in West Lebanon, New Hampshire. In 1978, they sold that store for $150,000 and moved to California.

After eight months, the Blanchards returned to the northeast, where they lived in a camper while Bob built a house in Vermont for them to live in.

In 1980, the Blanchards opened a toys and children's furniture store in New Hampshire, but in 1983, they decided to get out of that business too.

Meanwhile, Melinda had acquired a local reputation as a cook. Taking $2,000 from a $4,000 tax refund, they bought some jars and filled them with eight of Melinda's salad dressings, six dessert toppings, and 12 mustards. In May 1983, they took their sauces and dressings to the International Gourmet Products Show in San Francisco, and returned with 75 orders averaging $300 each.

Bob built some display racks for their products. Neighbors volunteered to fill the jars, label them, and pack them for shipping. Friends provided an additional $10,000 in financial support.

In August 1983, Blanchard & Blanchard & Son Ltd. exhibited at the New York Gift Show. This time, they received $45,000 worth of orders from such prominent retailers as Neiman-Marcus, Macy's and Marshall Field's.

Today, the Blanchards' company has a new headquarters building in Norwich, Vermont and employs 21 people. Sales amount to over $6 million a year.

Spouses ... and Co-Workers

A spouse's contributions to a fledgling business as a dedicated co-worker is another tale that is often repeated. In Skaneateles, New York, for example, Clara Clark has boned fish for 30 hours a week since she and her husband Doug opened Doug's Fish Fry in 1982. Their fish sandwich restaurant now has a dozen employees—and double that number during the summer.

When Henry Stickey started Western Medical Specialty Corp. on $2,000 from the family savings in 1978, his wife managed the desk, his daughter did the billing, and his son made the deliveries. The company now has 55 employees and annual sales of over $14 million.

When Steven Bursten started Decorating Den Systems Inc. in Indianapolis during the 1970s, his wife Valerie occasionally handled the phone, met customers at the airport, and filled in for the stock boy. But by the early 1980s, the Bursten children had grown so Valerie, a former TWA stewardess, took to the road selling franchises for the company. Now she trains all of the company's new franchisees—98 percent of whom are women.

_____ **FAMILY SUCCESS SCENARIO 25** _____

CONTINENTAL CAVIAR OF AMERICA INC.
Chattanooga, Tennessee

Although Laban DeFriese, a former Tennessee state representative, has developed his Chattanooga-based Continental Caviar of America Inc. into the largest producer of caviar in this country, it was his wife JoAnne who mixed up their first batch of caviar in the family garage.

Continental Caviar sells hackleback sturgeon and paddlefish caviar, purchased from back road fishermen who formerly threw it away or used it for catfish bait. Sales during 1987 were nearly $2 million.

While Laban sells the product, JoAnne serves as the company's Chief Executive Officer and supervises the five-employee processing plant.

Contributions Beyond Description

Sometimes, a spouse's contributions defy classification.

When Don Beaver needed to clean up a messy oil leak one day, for example, he took a pair of his wife's old pantyhose, filled them with kitty litter, and used them to soak up the oil.

Today, Beaver's New Pig Corp. sells thousands of "socks" filled with absorbent material to major industries, where they are used for cleaning up industrial spills.

One Spouse in Three
Gets Involved

Reliable figures regarding the participation of the family in operating a family business are not available, but in a 1986 study, one business publication reported that 33 percent of the spouses become involved, 28 percent of the children, 7 percent of the parents, 13 percent of the brothers, and 3 percent of the sisters. The study made no mention of in-laws.

_____ FAMILY SUCCESS SCENARIO 26 _____

AMERICAN BUILDERS & CONTRACTORS SUPPLY CO.
Beloit, Wisconsin

Ken Hendricks started American Builders & Contractors Supply in 1979. In 1983, he acquired three Midwestern roofing supply distributorships; in 1984, 13 East Coast distributorships; and in 1985, five Midwestern and eight Texas distributorships. By 1987, he had assembled a chain of 62 outlets in 26 states and was doing over $183 million a year in sales.

Hendricks' wife Diane handles all of the firm's legal and insurance affairs. His daughter Kendra handles centralized accounting and finance, while daughter Kimberlee is treasurer of the dealer supply division, and daughter Kathy installs computer systems for each of the distributorships.

A Partnership for Business Growth

Some wives like to handle the bookwork, some the "outside" work, such as sales, and some the "inside" work, including the office of chief executive officer. In whatever event, the number of spouses who become involved in the operation of family businesses is substantial.

_____ **FAMILY SUCCESS SCENARIO 27** _____

PACIFIC ENVELOPE/HALLMARK LITHO
Anaheim, California

Bob Cashman took over the bankrupt Pacific Envelope Co., almost $250,000 in debt, in 1975. Cashman taught himself the business while his wife Georgia ran the office and managed sales. Pacific Envelope began to grow.

In 1983, Cashman acquired Hallmark Litho, Inc., a foreclosed printing company, and Georgia took over the management of that.

By 1986, Pacific Envelope had captured 80 percent of the local market and was topping $10 million a year in sales. Hallmark Litho also was producing a healthy profit.

Women at the Helm

Traditionally, the male member of the household took the lead in starting up a family business. This was particularly true during the startup phase, when women often are busy managing the household and rearing the young children.

Even so, there are many instances in which it has been the women who have taken the initiative and who have gotten the family business going.

_____ **FAMILY SUCCESS SCENARIO 28** _____

CherAmi NATURAL PET FOODS
Larchmont, New York

Sharon Citrin, a former art teacher and gallery curator, loves animals, and in 1979, turned that interest into a business: CherAmi Natural Pet Foods.

Initially, Sharon spent her days baking animal biscuits and her nights driving around Manhattan with her husband to deliver the biscuits to pet stores, health food stores, and veterinarians' offices. In 1981, the Citrins sold $47,000 worth of Sharon's dog biscuits; in 1982, $100,000 worth.

In 1983, the Citrins arranged a $600,000 private placement through a Connecticut investment banking firm. The following year, backed by another $670,000 from private investors, they introduced their product to supermarkets across the country under the Good Nature brand name.

By 1985, CherAmi's sales had increased to $203,000, and in 1986, the company went public with a $1 million offering.

More Startups Today Are Due to
Women Than to Men

Small Business Administration figures show that, during a recent five-year period, twice as many women started businesses as men.

As much as ten years ago, there were 3.25 million small businesses in America owned by women, and that did not include those involved in partnerships, corporations, or farms.

Based on federal tax returns, some 2.9 million—or 24 percent—of the nation's partnerships, sole proprietorships, and Subchapter S corporations are headed by women.

_____ **FAMILY SUCCESS SCENARIO 29** _____

ANSA BOTTLE CO.
Muskogee, Oklahoma

In Muskogee, Oklahoma, Nickie Campbell managed a restaurant, and her husband Bill was vice president of a $15 million plumbing supply chain owned by his father.

The opportunity to start a business of their own arrived when the Campbells watched their infant son struggling to hold on to his bottle. Reasoning that a better design must be possible, Nickie and Bill turned to modeling clay and created a bottle that is shaped like a doughnut. It proved to be a great deal more manageable for infants to handle.

The Campbells mortgaged their house and cars to raise $250,000. With that, they formed Ansa Bottle Co. Inc. Nickie quit her job to work in the new company, but Bill retained his. As president of the young company, Nickie contacted representatives to sell their new bottle, and in August 1984 the first shipments were made. During the first three months, $60,000 worth of orders were received.

Bill quit his father's company and became Ansas's vice president.

In 1986, sales totaled $5 million and two new products were introduced.

Many Womens' Businesses Are Small

It is true that most companies headed by women are small. Indeed, in 1987 89.2 percent of them had only one paid employee. But statistics do not tell the whole story.

_____ **FAMILY SUCCESS SCENARIO 30** _____

MATANZAS CREEK WINERY
Sonoma County, California

Like the Campbells, Sandra MacIver found success in a bottle — in this case, a wine bottle.

MacIver founded Matanzas Creek winery in 1978.

Covering just 219 acres, only 45 of which are planted, Matanzas Creek is small, like Sandra herself (five-foot-one). Still, the winery produces 20,000 cases of choice wine per year.

Sandra's husband Bill is the winery's vice president and general manager.

Federal Law Assures Womens' Rights in Business

In the final months of President Reagan's administration, a law was passed to provide funds for giving management training and technical assistance to women business owners. The law also extends the protection of the 1974 Equal Opportunity Act to women, enabling them to obtain business loans more easily.

_____ **FAMILY SUCCESS SCENARIO 31** _____

OKLAHOMA CITY 89ers
Oklahoma City, Oklahoma

If women can be successful in wine making, why not baseball?

In Oklahoma, Patty Cox Hampton owns the Oklahoma City 89ers, a Triple A minor league baseball team. Not only is she the only woman to hold that distinction, she has handled the job well. The team was the runner-up for the American Association title in 1985, and Patty was named Executive of the Year by _The Sporting News_. In 1986, the 89ers produced $300,000 in profit on $2.5 million in revenue.

Patty Hampton didn't grow up in baseball. She married a doctor and bore four children before her marriage ended in divorce. Then she worked for an advertising agency and a public relations agency.

In the early 1970s, Hampton (then Cox) opened Cox Advertising Agency. In time, she hired Bing Hampton, whom she later would marry. The 89ers, which were owned by Harry Valentine, a wealthy Philadelphian, were one of Patty's advertising accounts.

Patty moved from advertising agent to general manager of the team. Then, when Valentine decided to sell the 89ers, a group of out-of-towners threatened to buy the team and move it out of town.

Patty mounted a media campaign to keep the team in Oklahoma City. She was successful in persuading several investors to help her buy the team for $100,000. Since then, the 89ers have become one of minor league baseball's most financially successful teams. Patty has had offers of $2 million to sell out.

Husband Bing is now the 89ers' executive vice president.

She Found a Segment of the Market and Staked a Claim

A substantial number of businesses owned by women cater to the female customer, which is not surprising. It is well recognized in retailing circles that women feel far more comfortable when shopping in a "man's" store than men do when shopping in a "woman's" store.

Regardless, an axiom in the business world since years gone by is one that says: Do the thing that you know best and shy away from the things that you know nothing about.

FAMILY SUCCESS SCENARIO 32

T. DEANE, INC.
Canton, Massachusetts

Trudy Sullivan spent 15 years as a woman's apparel buyer and manager for Boston department stores, and she was working for Filene's when she decided to open her own business.

She knew the market. Among the things that Sullivan had learned is that more than a third of the women in America, some 40 million of them, wear size 14 dresses or larger. In 1985, Sullivan raised $1.1 million from members of her family and opened a store to sell large-size designer apparel.

Over the next two years, Sullivan opened eight T. Deane, Inc. stores in Boston and in Connecticut. In 1987, she recorded $3 million in sales, with expectations of opening 18 more stores and reaching $17 million in sales the following year.

Entrepreneur's Divorce Rate Is Lower Than Average

Striving to establish a business can place a good deal of stress on any couple, but entrepreneurs' marriages seem to be exceptionally stable, according to New Enterprise Associates, a Baltimore-based venture capital firm. A study by New Enterprise found that the divorce rate of entrepreneurs is well below the national average.

A Checklist for Spouses in Business

To ensure the security of your family and the future of your business, there are certain common sense measures that both spouses should take.

Checking your life insurance program

Decide how much money your family will need if you die, then insure yourself accordingly. If other forms of life insurance are too expensive, consider term insurance.

Under certain circumstances, your insurance premiums can be paid for by the company, making the insurance — in effect — a tax-free fringe benefit.

Checking into your pension options

By federal law, both you and your spouse have control over the manner in which your pension benefits will be distributed.

Unless your spouse waives that right, on paper, your pension payments will automatically take the form of a joint and survivor annuity, meaning that one of you will receive reduced benefits after the other dies.

Investigate your other pension options.

Working out a partnership contract with your spouse

If your partner were *not* your spouse, you wouldn't hesitate to commit your agreement to writing. A businesslike contract with your spouse makes just as much sense: It provides protection for *both* parties.

Be sure to provide for the unfortunate possibility of divorce.

Where There's Stress, Divorce Always Threatens

Some family businesses fail, as anyone might expect — and some marriages collapse as well.

Whether or not the pressures of running a family business has been a contributing factor, a divorce can be a traumatic experience for anyone. After 17 years of marriage, Toby and David Feldman started a court reporting service in New York. Within a year, the couple separated, although both remained active in the business. After another year, the Feldmans divorced. They both continued to work in the business, however.

But after another two years, Toby had to call it quits, even though the company was bringing in about $1 million a year and it took legal assistance for her to dissolve the firm and start another company on her own.

A divorce generally makes an on-going relationship extremely difficult, particularly in the close confines of a shared office.

Rising Like a Phoenix from a Divorce

One of the critical aspects of a divorce is to determine a settlement that will allow both spouses to have enough financial security to build new lives for themselves.

FAMILY SUCCESS SCENARIO 33

LEAR'S
New York, New York

When Frances Lear launched *Lear's* magazine, she didn't need to shop around for a business loan.

Lear's is aimed at women over 40 who are executives or wives of executives—women whose household incomes exceed $40,000 a year—and Frances is the former wife of television producer Norman Lear.

After 28 years of marriage, the Lears divorced—and Frances got a multimillion-dollar settlement. That settlement enabled Frances to spend two and one-half years studying the publishing industry, then invest $25 million on founding *Lear's*.

Lear's appeared as a bimonthly publication in 1988 and became a monthly in 1990.

Retirees Are Starting Family Businessess Too

A couple of years ago, *Industry Week* magazine surveyed a number of management-level people between the ages of 45 and 54 about their plans for retirement. The findings: 16 percent said that they would *start a new career* and an additional 17 percent said specifically that they would *go into business* after they retire.

Widows Must Be Prepared to Carry on

It is a fact of life that, on average, women outlive men, and it is an unfortunate extension of that fact that women will have to take over many of their families' obligations in later life after their husbands have gone.

This may mean that, while men are retiring at an ever earlier age, women may have to work even longer.

_____ **FAMILY SUCCESS SCENARIO 34** _____

LOS TIOS
Houston, Texas

Rosemary Garbett of Houston married while she was only a teen-ager. Her husband Thomas was a capable but autocratic man who started a Tex-Mex restaurant named Los Tios (The Uncles) in 1970. Early on, Rosemary helped out as a cashier or by keeping the books.

By 1975, Thomas had opened three restaurants in the Houston area, but by the following year he was dead. For months, Garbett's estate was tied up in appraisal, along with his insurance. When an offer was received from a group that wished to buy the restaurants for 50 cents on the dollar, Rosemary refused.

A manager, a top chef, and four office workers left.

Suppliers began to demand cash on delivery.

Rosemary discovered that some of her husband's employees had been stealing food and money.

Taking control of the restaurants, Rosemary set up a system of internal controls.

She instituted an open door policy for employees.

She delegated full authority to each restaurant manager—and gave each one a share of the profits.

Within a year, Rosemary had her debt under control and saw her margins climbing.

She instituted an eight-week training program for the employ-ees and developed a policy manual.

She established a central warehouse and central purchasing to control inventory and earn bulk discounts from suppliers.

She set up central kitchens and bought a fleet of trucks to de-liver the prepared food to the restaurants.

Rosemary personally reads every customer comment card, ap-proves every invoice, and signs every check.

She started a new tortilla company to assure consistent product quality, and she has developed a totally new market: Kraft, Inc. is now distributing her Los Tios line.

Rosemary has added four new restaurants since her husband's death. She is considering the franchise field, and also is thinking about taking the company public.

Widows Must Be Prepared for Business

In the early 1950s, fewer than 30 percent of the women between 55 and 64 were working, but by 1988 that figure was nearing 50 percent. Few of these women, unfortunately, will be capable of taking the reins of a thriving business; in fact, the U.S. Census Bureau says that 80 percent of America's retired women *are not eligible for pensions* and have a median income of just $5,616 a year!

_____ **FAMILY SUCCESS SCENARIO 35** _____

CRAIN COMMUNICATIONS, INC.
Chicago, Illinois

In 1936, Gertrude Ramsey, an executive secretary at NBC in Chicago, met G. D. Crain Jr., head of Crain Communications, Inc. At 51, Crain was twice Gertrude's age, but they married and produced two sons.

Gertrude was made assistant treasurer of the company in 1942 and secretary treasurer in 1949 after the Crain sons had become teenagers.

In 1973, G. D. died, and Gertrude took the reins.

Aided by her two sons, Keith and Rance, Gertrude (81 in 1991) has advanced Crain Communications from five publications to 26, from 100 employees to over 1,000, and from less than $10 million in gross revenues to over $120 million.

Chapter 5 Checkup

For Your Spouse

	Yes	No
1. Do you help your spouse around the house?	_____	_____
2. Do you help your spouse at work?	_____	_____
3. Do you make it a point to keep your spouse informed about major business situations?	_____	_____
4. If you were laid up, or otherwise incapacitated, would your wife have the information and the business skills to carry on?	_____	_____

If the answer to any of these questions has been no, prepare a plan to correct the situation as quickly as possible.

6
Children: Do as You Say... or Do as You Do?

If you want an instant ulcer, try to tell other people how to raise their children. (I prefer to leave that aggravation to the child psychologists and family counselors.) Still, the parent-child relationship is frequently at the heart of a family business:

- The ones who start a business often are motivated by a desire to "prove themselves" to their parents, to their children, or to some other member(s) of the family.

- The desire to succeed is stimulated, in large part, by a wish to provide a comfortable standard of living for one's self, one's spouse, and one's children.

- Many entrepreneurs share the dream of building a strong, profitable business that they eventually can pass along to their children.

Good Intentions Are Not Enough

It is interesting to note that only 30 percent of the family businesses— less than one out of three—actually pass on to the second generation; and only 10 percent—one out of ten—are passed along to the *third* generation.

These are shockingly low percentages, but there are a number of reasons for them. Most of those reasons have no bearing on the type of relationship that the business owners have (or have had) with their children. A myriad of other things—unexpected things—can occur, such as:

- Some businesses will fail, unfortunately, leaving nothing to pass along to the next generation.

- The owner-founder may sell or liquidate the business before it can be passed along.

- New technology may make the business obsolete between one generation and the next.

- The children may prefer careers of another nature and have no desire to run the family business.

- Some children simply *do not have the ability* to take over a business and operate it.

- If there are a large number of children in the family, the business *may not be able* to support them all.

I'm sure you can think of other reasons that could be added to this list. Each situation calls for a different approach—perhaps an adjustment in attitude, or even a change in the way you choose to build and manage your business.

Early Training Is the Key to Successful Careers

Picture a world class athlete like Boris Becker. When Becker first learned how to play tennis, it was an enormous thrill to discover that there were some people that he could beat. From then on, he kept striving to beat better and better players; and when there no longer were any amateurs capable of beating him, he turned professional, moving to an even higher level of competition. Finally, as his ability was raised to the limit, he competed in—and won—The Wimbledon.

So it is in life; and as it is in life, it is in business.

It is important to realize that Boris Becker did not simply pick up a tennis racquet and a short time later storm onto the tennis court at Wimbledon. He had to be trained, he had to begin with a series of lesser victories—and some defeats—along the way.

Parents must realize that their children have to develop their talents gradually, win a few small victories to build their confidence, and be allowed to have an occasional failure while they are learning the family business.

Children Must Learn to Succeed

Success is not something that is transmitted through the genes; it is something that must be *learned*. And the "tutors" must be not only competent, but patient and understanding as well.

In learning how to succeed, we must learn how to disagree. This isn't always easy within a family. Parents have a natural tendency to shelter their children from worry, and children have an equally strong tendency to avoid confronting their parents.

But if one's children are to join the family business, it is important (a) that the parents give them *all* the facts with which to make informed decisions, and (b) that the parents allow—and even *encourage*—their children to question, challenge, dare to seek newer, better, more efficient, more profitable ways of handling their business-related chores.

Parents can serve as living examples that:

- Following one's instincts alone can be risky.

- Consistently attempting to overpower one's opposition can be dangerous.

- Nothing in business—or in life—can be more deadly than simply maintaining the status quo.

- Allies can accomplish things, while enemies simply destroy.

_____ **FAMILY SUCCESS SCENARIO 36** _____

MOLEX, INC.
Lisle, Illinois

One father who saw that his children developed a solid business background early is John Krehbiel Sr., chairman of Molex, Inc. in Lisle, Illinois. As a matter of fact, when Krehbiel's sons, John Jr. and Frederick, first said that they would like to work at Molex, their father found the lowest-paid employee in the company, and paid his sons a dollar an hour *less*.

Molex is the world's third largest producer of electronic connections. It grew out of a substance developed by John Sr.'s father, F. A. Krehbiel—a material created from cold tar pitch and asbestos, waste materials that are discarded by other companies. The elder Krehbiel found that the substance had good electrical properties and offered excellent moisture resistance. He built his first plant in Brookfield, Illinois in 1938, and his first Molex products were toy guns and submarines. The first commercial use for his new material was in fabricating a pipe for use in drawing cable through manholes. Later it was used for farm drain tiles.

Sales finally took off, however, when electrical companies began to order T- and L-shaped connectors made out of Molex.

Meanwhile, John Krehbiel Sr. had started his own business, J. H. Krehbiel Co., to manufacture electrical insulation. That plant burned down, however, so John Sr. decided to work with his father at Molex. Since then, the company has grown tremendously.

Molex now produces over 25,000 products, has 39 plants on six continents, and generates some $500 million a year in sales.

As for John Sr.'s sons, who truly started on the bottom rung of the company ladder, John Jr. now serves as president of Molex and Frederick serves as president of Molex International.

Training the Children as Successors Can Be a Full-Time Job

A number of colleges and universities now offer courses—and even full programs—on how to manage a family business. What one learns from one's parents is even more important because their experience is directly transferable, not some abstract "for instance" contained in a college textbook. Realistically, however, even those who may have the talent for it (and few people do) do not have the time and energy to run a business *and* tutor their children concurrently.

_____ **FAMILY SUCCESS SCENARIO 37** _____

CAPSCO SALES, INC.
Sunnyvale, California

One entrepreneurial parent who wants her children to be fully prepared to take her place in the family business is Billye Ericksen-Desaigoudar.

Ericksen-Desaigoudar also knows that mother isn't necessarily the best teacher!

Four years after Ericksen-Desaigoudar joined Capsco, a distributor of electronic components, she took over the company in a $1.2 million leveraged buyout. At the time, Capsco's sales were $6 million a year; now they have reached $20 million a year.

Two sons and a daughter are involved in their mother's business—Ken, Kirk, and Kathy. Each was already getting a good amount of first-hand experience at Capsco, but their mother didn't think that the training she could give them would be good enough. So, to expand her children's training, Ericksen-Desaigoudar appointed a board of directors comprised of top managers from various segments of the electronics industry.

The forward-looking mother told the new directors that she was eventually planning to step aside, letting her successors take over after a leveraged buyout. She said that she had selected five top managers from within Capsco, including her three children, to carry on, and that she would like each director to give each of those managers six weeks of solid training within their companies during the next several years.

In exchange for this service, Ericksen-Desaigoudar told the board, she would compensate each of them on a quarterly basis throughout the training period and would give each director a share of the buyout price when that event occurred.

Ericksen-Desaigoudar realized that this approach could create some problems among her other employees, who might feel that they would have no future with Capsco unless they were one of the five hand-picked trainees. Her response was to draw up an organization chart that pinpointed 14 key positions that would need to be filled when the company reached $20 million a year in sales.

The $20 million figure was the target—and the incentive. Since there are only three Ericksen-Desaigoudars and 14 key positions to be filled, the other employees would have ll positions to vie for.

It was a plan that contained something for everyone—and it gave Ericksen-Desaigoudar's children the opportunity to learn the business from some of the finest tutors that the industry has to offer.

Daughters Can Make Contributions as Well as Sons

Robin Bacci put in a long apprenticeship at the family's San Rafael, California automobile business before taking over from her father Roland. Since then, Robin has created a new team of sales, service, and parts managers, and has increased sales at the Mercedes-Benz dealership by 25 percent a year.

Another daughter who has left her mark on the family business is Betsy Kasper.

_____ FAMILY SUCCESS SCENARIO 38 _____

KASPER FOUNDRY CO.
Elyria, Ohio

A third-generation family business, Kasper Foundry Co., like most old foundries, was dirty, poorly lit, hot in the summer, cold in the winter, and staffed by blue collar workers who swear, sweat, and spit on the floor. At least they did, until Betsy Kasper joined the firm.

Betsy served an apprenticeship under a stern taskmaster—her

father—but within a year, she knew the name of every employee. The men began to accept her. And she began to act on some of the things that her own observations told her needed to be done.

Betsy advised employees of the hazardous chemicals that are used in the shop (an OSHA requirement).

She had the cafeteria painted.

She promoted the company basketball games.

But most important, she created the firm's first quality control manual, as a result of which Kasper Foundry can now compete for government contracts.

Daughters Frequently Are More People-Oriented

The ability to deal with people—family, employees, customers, suppliers, competitors, and what have you—is a valuable asset to anyone in business.

For whatever reason, women often are better at dealing with people than are men, as Arnold Daniels found out in his business.

_____ FAMILY SUCCESS SCENARIO 39 _____

PRAENDEX, INC.
Boston, Massachusetts

In 1956, Arnold Daniels organized Praendex, Inc., a management and organizational development firm. Over the years, he and his wife raised three children, two sons, and a daughter, and the business grew to $4 million a year in sales.

But Daniels was a lone wolf—hard working, but strong willed and reluctant to develop an organization or to delegate responsibility. When his sons, Arnie Jr. and Stephen, joined the company in the 1970s, they found that they couldn't work with their father.

"I was looking for somebody who would do exactly what I do, the way I do it," admits Daniels.

The boys were too independent to work that way. They had their own ideas. They wanted to leave their own brand on the business, not just mimic their father. Both left the company, only to rejoin it, leave it again, and join it a third time.

Dinah, Daniels' daughter, is the youngest of the three children. She had worked in the family business as a secretary while in high school, but later became a secretary for the Boston Symphony Orchestra. From there, Dinah had risen to the position of public relations director, and then had gone on to similar posts with other prominent orchestras. She also had married.

In 1986, Daniels—by then past 65—realized that both he and his business needed help. He offered the presidency to Dinah, and she, at the urging of her husband, accepted.

Dinah has provided the "bridge" that holds the company—and the family—together. She can work with her father *and* with her brothers. Arnie Jr. likes to work on the technical aspects of the business; Stephen has a flair for sales.

Dinah has improved the firm's marketing efforts, improved relationships with their 22 licensees, doubled the size of their office, and increased the profitability of their operations. And her father has the satisfaction of knowing that, once he steps aside, his company will be in good hands.

Children Bring Many Benefits to a Business

When children *do* enter the family business, they often contribute a lot:

A youthful point of view

Enthusiasm

Ideas involving new concepts, new technologies, or new products

Maurice Lee Jr. gave up a job as an engineer at Douglas Aircraft to help his father start Smokorama, which manufactures pressurized barbecue cookers for hotels and food chains. By 1988, the firm had 25 employees and sales of over $3 million a year.

New Blood, Fresh Ideas

Where many businesses tend to fall into a rut—even grow stodgy—over the years, the participation of succeeding generations can help to eliminate that tendency.

_____ **FAMILY SUCCESS SCENARIO 40** _____

VOCATIONAL TRAINING CENTER
St. Louis, Missouri

After Marshall Lasky's son Steven joined the family's Vocational Training Center in St. Louis, revenues increased 15-fold in six years. Profits increased 15 percent.

The elder Lasky opened his TV repair shop after graduating from college and at night began to train other men in his back room. A year later, he formed VTC. Lasky's wife Jeanette worked in the company, and sons Steven and Edward pitched in part time.

It was five years before the company began to make a profit. VTC inched ahead, training 250 students a year—mostly blue collar workers who had lost jobs in the St. Louis auto plants and were looking for a new occupation.

In 1980, Steven—who had become a high school coach—quit his coaching job and joined the family business. Steven immediately began to target a new market for VTC—the job-poor residents of the inner city ghettos. After that, he restructured the company's class offerings so that they would match the community's best employment opportunities by providing training for such jobs as nurse's assistant and data entry operator. Next he opened schools in the inner city neighborhoods, where they would be more accessible to VTC's clientele.

Within six years, the Laskys' company had expanded from one school to eight, from 250 students to 1,400, from a staff of 12 to a staff of nearly 300, and from $237,000 a year in revenues to $9 million.

New Blood, New Energy

There are countless other stories of how the second generation has taken a family business and steered it in a new direction. One such story involves Blue Ridge Farms.

─────────── **FAMILY SUCCESS SCENARIO 41** ───────────

BLUE RIDGE FARMS, INC.
Brooklyn, New York

Blue Ridge was founded by Seymour Siegel. Its products were prepared deli salads, and it was a $4 million business before Siegel's son Jeff joined the company. But Jeff knew that his parents' company could do better.

Like the children of many entrepreneurs, Jeff started at the bottom—working in the Blue Ridge kitchens. Gradually, he learned more about the way the business was run, and he soon realized that 80 percent of the company's business was done with one customer, on a handshake basis, without a contract.

Jeff set out to find some new accounts. During the next five years, he not only located new accounts, but added several new products to the Blue Ridge line.

Sales and profits increased by 20 to 30 percent a year. Jeff spent a few thousand dollars on radio advertising, and sales increased even more. After that, it was television advertising and another increase in sales.

Today, Jeff Siegel is senior vice president in charge of sales at Blue Ridge, the company sells its products in 30 states, plus Canada, and annual revenues top $50 million.

New Blood, New Products

One of the hallmarks of a good leader is a visionary outlook: "How can I do this better than I'm doing it now?"

Each generation, ideally, has "something new" to add to the family business. This should be encouraged because that is how businesses keep up with the times, grow, diversify, stay competitive.

Too many people who have founded a company find this sort of thing threatening. They feel comfortable doing things "the old way." They are unwilling to change.

Henry Ford produced black cars with four-cylinder engines for far too long. Had he not finally been convinced to change his point of view, the company eventually would have foundered.

_____ FAMILY SUCCESS SCENARIO 42 _____

SPECIALTY EQUIPMENT CORP.
Worcester, Massachusetts

Specialty Equipment Corp. was founded in the mid-1950s by Dave Dowd. The company manufactures machines to make corrugated boxes.

When Dave Dowd's son Fred became president of the company in the mid-1970s, the firm was selling fewer than five machines a year. About that time, however, Weyerhaeuser Co. contacted the firm regarding a machine that could manufacture self-locking cartons that could be assembled by a worker in the field.

Specialty Equipment developed the Sec-Loc Finishing System, and quickly sold 15 machines at half a million dollars each. But Fred felt that the company was capable of doing more.

The Dowds exchanged 12.5 percent of their stock for $1 million in cash and loan guarantees from a Boston venture capital firm. With that money, they built a series of small box making plants in selected areas around the country. Each $2 million plant produces about $10 million a year in sales.

The new venture put the Dowds in competition with some of their traditional customers, but Fred felt that there would be no serious repercussions from it for three reasons:

1. Each plant is aiming for a limited market—less than one percent of the potential in its region—in which the buyers include mostly farmers, meat and fish packers, and warehousers.

2. By demonstrating the value of the Sec-Loc Finishing System, Dowd expects other box makers to want to buy their equipment.

3. Down the road, Specialty Equipment may sell its box making *plants* and return exclusively to the manufacture of box making *equipment*, leaving the actual making of boxes to their traditional customers.

But for the time being, the Dowds have expanded into a new phase of their family-owned enterprise, realizing that flexibility is the surest way to achieve growth.

Building a Family Dynasty

Good training "at the knee of one's father" has often led to the creation of a great family dynasty. Years ago, the Rockefeller fortunes were created; more recently, the Pritzkers'. Less familiar, perhaps, is the story of Chicago's Wexler family.

_____ **FAMILY SUCCESS SCENARIO 43** _____

JUPITER INDUSTRIES
Chicago, Illinois

Jerry Wexler "learned at the knee" of his father Simon, whose business acumen resulted in part or total ownership of 16 companies including Allied Radio Corp., an enormous retail and catalog supply firm that Simon sold to Tandy Corp. in the 1960s.

After marrying the daughter of a prominent Chicago real estate magnate, Jerry Wexler became first a real estate broker and then a partner in his in-laws' firm. But five years later, he found another partner in plumber- engineer-developer Edward Ross, and struck out on his own by forming Jupiter Industries.

Since the early 1950s, Wexler and Ross have built a $3 billion empire that includes real estate, construction, retailing, trucking, manufacturing, and finance. Among the two dozen hotels that the duo own are Chicago's Drake, Ambassador West, Executive House, and Oxford House. Their interests range from coast to coast, and Wexler's own net worth is estimated at more than $250 million.

It Takes Time to Build a Dynasty

Jerry Wexler gained a great deal of his business acumen from his father and father-in-law.

_____ FAMILY SUCCESS SCENARIO 44 _____

PRINCE MACARONI CO.
Lowell, Massachusetts

J. P. Pellegrino, who immigrated to the United States at the age of 12, learned his business from an Italian uncle.

In 1932, Pellegrino married into the Realmuto family in Manhattan, where the Realmutos operated a family business called Roman Macaroni Co. Pellegrino bought a piece of the firm for $12,500, and within six months became the company's top salesman. Within a year, he was running the firm.

In 1940, Pellegrino bought out his wife's uncle for $125,000 and took over the business. A few months later, his factory burned down.

Meanwhile, in Lowell, Massachusetts, a trio of Sicilian immigrants—Michele Cantella, Gaetano LaMarca, and Guiseppe Seminara—were operating the Prince Co., another regional pasta maker. Pellegrino learned that Prince was not doing well—in fact, it was $300,000 in debt and losing an additional $5,000 a month. So he made an unusual offer: If he could make the business profitable in a month, the owners would sell him one-fourth of the company's stock for $50,000 and negotiate a voting trust agreement that would give Pellegrino control over production and sales.

During his first month, Pellegrino produced a $900 profit, and earned a position as one of the company's partners.

The Pellegrino/Realmuto family moved to Andover, Massachusetts—J.P., his wife, and their young son Joseph; J.P.'s mother-in-law; and four unmarried sisters-in-law. The sisters-in-law soon went to work for the company, and J.P. soon bought out two of his partners, LaMarca and Seminara.

Between 1940 and 1950, Prince's sales grew from $5 million a year to $10 million. Over the next two decades, he expanded through a succession of acquisitions—Cleghorn Container Co., Viviano Macaroni Co. of St. Louis, Roselli Foods of New Jersey, Meisenzahl Macaroni Co. of Rochester, Cardinale Macaroni Co. of Brooklyn, Roma Macaroni of Chicago, Michigan Macaroni of Detroit. By 1959, Prince's sales had risen to $22 million.

J.P.'s son Joe grew, graduated from college, served as an officer in the Marines, married, and had a child of his own before entering the business. There, he worked in the plant during the day, and studied accounting and management at night. Within 18 months, he became the plant manager.

Young Joe recognized many of the company's weaknesses—small run-down plants, poor management, serious debts, and a plethora of little known brands. He merged two weak Michigan companies into one—Prince Macaroni of Michigan. He began to produce private label products. He began to pay incentive bonuses to key executives. Now Prince's executive vice president, he saw the company's sales rise from $27 million in 1969 to $29 million in 1970. Profits rose from $1 million to $1.3 million.

In 1973, young Joe was promoted to president. J.P. remained active as chairman.

Stepping from One Success to Another

Sometimes the family business provides the next generation with a steppingstone toward success in some other direction.

David Eidenberg went straight from college to General Store Fixture Co., a firm that was established by his grandfather in the 1920s and is now headed by his father. But in 1986, Eidenberg struck off on his own to form Food Service Co., which now competes with the original family business in designing and equipping restaurants.

In a similar fashion, Peter Morton stepped out of the family's highly successful fourth-generation restaurant business in Chicago to start a successful restaurant chain of his own: the Hard Rock Cafes.

A Good Name Can Be a Valuable Asset

Sometimes, a family's reputation, rather than its money, can provide a springboard to new business opportunities.

_____ **FAMILY SUCCESS SCENARIO 45** _____

FLIGHT INTERNATIONAL GROUP
Atlanta, Georgia

Doug Matthews' father was an Air Force colonel and President Dwight D. Eisenhower's personal pilot.

Matthews himself got a pilot's license at the age of 16. At the U.S. Naval Academy, he earned a degree with honors in aeronautical engineering. During the Vietnam War, he received two Bronze Stars, 11 Air Medals, and a Purple Heart while flying 155 combat missions. And after the war, he became a pilot for Delta Airline.

In 1976, seeing that other pilots needed training to fly the Boeing 727, Matthews saw an opportunity to go into business. With a $2,000 investment, he rented an office, took out ads, and printed a textbook. Soon, 1,500 pilots a year were paying him between $250 and $15,000 apiece to take his courses.

In 1983, Matthews quit Delta to become the full-time president of Flight International. A year later, he formed Intercredit, an airliner leasing company that he soon sold for a $700,000 profit. He also sold his Boeing 727 training school for $150,000 profit and formed Flight International Airlines, a charter service that quickly folded.

Matthews took his business public, selling 500,000 shares—a quarter of the company—at $8.50 a share.

Since he had personally participated in training flights while in the Navy, Matthews knew that it costs about $8,000 an hour for the military to use its own pilots and planes during war games exercises. In 1980, he convinced the government that he could provide the service for $2,500 an hour—resulting in $25 million worth of government contracts.

In 1987, Matthews acquired a five-year, $97 million Air Force contract, and a four-year, $28-million contract from the Federal Reserve Bank in Boston, which hired Matthews' company to deliver checks overnight among the bank's 12 banking districts.

Now Matthews is the owner of one of the world's largest private air fleets. His company has annual revenues of some $50 million and a net income of some $750,000.

Family Businesses Often Begin with the Children

The ways in which family businesses originate are countless. Some of them begin as a business partnership between a parent and a child. One such company is Snoozy's Room in Sunnyvale, California.

Snoozy's Room was founded by Barbara Patton and her mother, both of whom put a few thousand dollars into the business to get it going. The first product was a child's hand-sewn stuffed clown. Other products were added as sales grew. Today, looking at a $10- to $15-million business, daughter Barbara still cuts the cloth and handles the shipping, but home workers do the sewing on a piecework basis.

A similar startup created Suburban Satellite Systems of Harrisburg, Pennsylvania. Although James Finn, who started the company in 1987, serves as the Chief Executive Officer, his mother owns 40 percent of the stock and occupies a seat on the board of directors.

If the Firm Benefits, the Children Often Benefit More

Children receive a variety of benefits from working in a family business, whether or not they eventually take over from their parents. Among the many important lessons that they can learn are to:

Appreciate the value of money.

Pick up valuable management skills.

Develop the type of discipline required to successfully run a company.

Assume responsibility.

Delegate responsibility.

Respect the contributions made by others.

Offspring can also earn spending money and save for a college education while working in the family business.

Working Flexible Hours Can Help Young and Old

Children often can arrange to work flexible hours in the family business—hours that are convenient to their classroom schedules and to their extracurricular activities while they are still in school.

After the children have grown, are married, and have children of their own, flexible hours can be arranged to accommodate their family routines, their spouses' schedules, or their children's schedules once the children have reached school age.

Later in life, the seniors may find it convenient to work flexible hours, coasting into their retirement and gradually easing the control of the family business into the hands of the next generation.

Few companies are as likely to let an employee work flexible hours as a family business.

_____ **FAMILY BUSINESS SCENARIO 46** _____

IDENTIFICATION SERVICES, INC.
Minneapolis, Minnesota

Beverly Napurski has two small children, but she is able to fill the position of vice president of finance in her mother's company because she can work flexible hours.

Beverly's mother, Christine Johnson, started Identification Services, Inc. in her home and built it into a $1-million-a-year business manufacturing signs, caps, jackets, and name badges.

Beverly manages the company's finances, and her father Elert has resigned his position in a local computer company to serve as president of the firm.

Not Everyone Is a Self-Starter

Many of the offspring described in this chapter are obviously self-starters, eager to join the family business and make it grow. These children are largely self-motivated, personally talented, and individually ambitious. As every parent knows, not all children are like that.

Some children need other motivation. Some even need outright *prodding* to develop their latent skills, to establish a set of goals, and to formulate a "game plan" for getting where they want to go in life.

Growing up is not easy. To some, a successful parent is a ready-made role model; to others, the successful parent is "bigger than life" and represents a challenge that children feel they are incapable of handling.

_____ **FAMILY SUCCESS SCENARIO 47** _____

FROM THE HEART, INC.
Tucson, Arizona

Kevin Kelly studied Russian and Soviet Studies at the University of Arizona, but he also handled most of the business matters for From the Heart, Inc., a company that his mother founded in 1983.

From the Heart bakes chocolate chip cookies, attaches them to plastic stems with silk leaves, and packages them to look like a dozen long-stemmed roses in a clear plastic floral box, tied with a large red ribbon.

Barbara Kelly developed the idea for From the Heart when she produced the first "roses" as a gift for her mother's 72nd birthday. Soon, the cookies were being produced by a bakery in New York as well as Tucson, and 14 distributors were scattered across the country.

In 1986, From the Heart sold its first franchise.

Today, the Tucson store sells over 5,000 boxes of cookies a year, and Barbara Kelly's creations are featured by such well-known retailers as Neiman-Marcus, Bloomingdale's, and Pepperidge Farm.

Kevin Kelly, still in his twenties, is president of the company, and his brother Tim works there too.

Children Need Challenges...
and Support

Children *need* challenges, but they also need reassurance. It is one thing
to set a lofty goal for your children, but you also need to provide a series
of lesser goals along the way—goals that are within their reach, so that
they can feel the encouragement of accomplishments as they grow in
self-confidence.

By making each subgoal a little more difficult to attain than the one
before, you expand your children's capabilities, stretch their talents, extend their horizons, and increase their willingness to face the next challenge that may come along.

_____ **FAMILY SUCCESS SCENARIO 48** _____

SIRRAH
New York, New York

When Abe Harris founded the Peter Pan chain of dress shops in
1925, for example, it was his intention to sell middle-of-the-line
cotton frocks. The chain grew to include 60 stores.

By 1947, with Abe's sons Jerome and Lester now involved in the
business, the family realized that the garment industry was changing. As a result, the family sold off most of the stores, moved into
direct marketing, and began to produce its own dresses.

In 1947, the industry went through additional changes. This time,
the Harris family made a difficult decision and decided to sell out.
Now, with his share of the proceeds, Jerome Harris has founded a
new business: an international business brokerage firm called Sirrah.

A Job in the Family Business
Isn't Always the Answer

Entrepreneur Gary Amato has his own view of succession. He doesn't
want to burden his son with a hand-me-down family business.

"I'd be much happier," says Amato, "if I could build a successful business now so that someday I can say to my son: 'Here's a million dollars;
do what you want with it.'"

_____ **FAMILY SUCCESS SCENARIO 49** _____

ALLINE LAMINATED PRODUCTS, INC.
Cleveland, Ohio

Frank Amato and a partner founded Alline Laminated Products,
Inc. in 1963 as a job shop to manufacture kitchen cabinets. Their

product was built with hammer and nails, and their business operated on a cash basis.

By 1971, Alline was a company with six employees and $150,000 a year in sales.

Frank's son Gary helped out in his father's shop as a youngster, then went to college for a degree in business. In 1971, he was looking forward to a career as a stockbroker. But that was the year Frank's partner announced that he would like to sell out.

Gary knew that his father needed help. He knew, too, that the family business was nearly bankrupt. And he also thought he knew what had to be done:

Create a product line.

Develop a sales organization.

Gradually build up the company's manufacturing capacity using newer and more modern techniques.

Gary began by getting a $68,000 loan to buy out Frank's old partner.

He spent his days making cabinets and his evenings driving from contractor to contractor in order to sell them.

Gary put all of the profits, along with money from additional loans, into buying new equipment. In 1978, he persuaded his father to sell out, giving him full control of the company. Frank received double the book value of the firm, paid out over a seven-year period.

Gary then began to work harder than before, and Alline inched ahead.

Unable to afford a full-time salesperson, Gary took on some sales representatives. He developed a board of advisers, and hired an accountant and an attorney.

By 1986, Alline had 70 employees, and sales topping $4 million.

Discipline Can Create Dilemmas

When a family works together in a business, discipline sometimes can be a problem. It is easy—and often tempting—to comingle one's family life and one's business life. One should take care to avoid that.

If a child misbehaves at home, discipline him at home; and if she misbehaves at work, discipline her at work. It may seem expedient to tell your son: "You stayed out too late last night, so today I'm going to make you clean up the stock room," or to tell your daughter: "You didn't handle the Miller order correctly, so I'll expect you to wash the dishes after dinner."

Both of those are the wrong approach. The boy violated a *household* rule by staying out too late, so tell *him* to wash the dinner dishes. The girl violated a *business* rule by mishandling the Miller order, so tell *her* to clean up the stock room.

The discipline should fit the situation, and if it doesn't, the child receives a mixed set of signals.

Punishment Can Be Hard to Administer

Punishment at home for poor behavior at work can result in an unending series of conflicts and tensions within the family. No matter what happens at work, children need to know that they are loved and appreciated in the home.

Similarly, punishing a child at work for something that has happened in the home can be a big turn-off as far as the child's attitude toward the business is concerned. The feeling might be, "If they're going to hassle me at work, why should I bother working? Who needs it?"

Where children are concerned, it is always a good idea to be overly conservative, rather than overly critical.

We have heard many comments along the lines of, "He cares more about his darned business than he does about me!" or "She treats the people at work better than she treats me!" True or not, that is how those children viewed the situation, and the result was friction within the family. Antipathy, if not total resentment, may arise toward the family business along with a somewhat unstable, albeit aggravating, tendency for the children to reject both.

Make It Clear That the Home Is the Home

By maintaining a clear separation between the home and the business, you provide your children with an alternative. "I made a mistake at work, but I'll make it up to my parents when we get home" is a natural way for children to win back your favor, as well as for you to demonstrate your parental understanding and compassion for them.

These are the things that strengthen the bonds between parents and their children. Without them, children often feel compelled to look elsewhere for that understanding.

A Reward Is a Double-Edged Sword

Like discipline, rewards need to be handled carefully where one's children are involved. But since rewards are generally a positive experience, they are less likely to generate negative repercussions.

Notice the words "less likely," because there are indeed times when a reward can create problems. For example, when:

- An act by one child earns a reward, but the same act by another child does not.
- A small act receives a large reward, and a big act receives a small reward.
- You reward an employee for some act that does not produce a similar reward for one of your children.
- You reward an act on one occasion, but not on the next.

Not All Good Deeds Deserve a Reward

Children—and employees, for that matter—need to clearly understand which deeds merit a reward and which ones do not. One clearly should *not* be rewarded for the normal execution of assigned duties. Rewards should be reserved for extraordinary, not ordinary, performance.

Children—and employees—also need to know *what kind* of reward they can expect. If the reward doesn't seem to equal the effort expended, it will be resented, rather than appreciated.

Sometimes, a Poorly Conceived Reward Can Backfire

There is a "flip side" to this situation. Just as a child (or an employee) can react negatively when improperly rewarded, so can the person who is attempting to reward someone feel that the gesture is not appreciated. It is an awkward, even ridiculous, sort of scenario.

For example, an employee does something extraordinary, and the boss gives her a small bonus.

Instead of feeling good about the reward, the employee feels slighted and underappreciated. Her feelings are reflected in her voice, her manner, and her subsequent performance.

The boss senses her disappointment and feels that she is unappreciative and overly demanding. After all, the boss didn't *have* to give her *anything*! Hadn't he *tried* to be nice?

His resentment grows... and so does hers.

"After all, it's *his* fault. I did a darned good job!"

Oh, really?

"It's clearly *her* fault. I tried to do something nice to show her my appreciation, but it just wasn't good enough for her!"

She finds another job and quits, or he gets so frustrated by the situation that he lets her go. Either way, she has lost a good job and he has lost a valuable employee.

Both parties lose.

Don't automatically assume that a spontaneous act of generosity will encourage and stimulate your children or your employees.

Think your policies through, and explain them to everyone in detail. Most particularly, implement them fairly and consistently at all times.

Promotions: Some Win Them, Some Don't

Another area of potential difficulty comes when a promotion is announced in the firm.

If you promote one of your children over others from outside the family, you run the risk of alienating a large percentage of your work force. If you promote an "outsider" over one of your children, you run the risk of alienating a member (or members) of your family.

Promotions are another form of reward, and should be approached in the same manner. Create a promotion policy, explain it fully, and implement it fairly and consistently. Under those circumstances, your decision will be easier to make, easier to justify, and easier for everyone concerned to understand.

Even so, try to make some accommodation for also-rans—the ones who *almost* got the job, but didn't. An increase in salary is probably fitting. After all, the also-rans were strong competitors for promotion and hence valuable employees, so you want to keep them around. They'll still feel badly about missing a chance for promotion, but the raise will ease the blow.

Everyone Should Compete for a Worthy Goal

Competition is healthy as long as the objectives are worthwhile, the rivalry is clean and fair, and the contestants remain friends and allies, win or lose.

Parents should challenge their children—a form of competition within the family. And since the parents cannot personally engage in every facet of their children's lives, they can and should encourage competition between their children, between the children and their friends, and at work between the children and the other employees.

The important thing is to be sure that they compete fairly, compete for worthwhile causes, and know that *it is OK to fail* from time to time.

Sibling Rivalry Is Natural, But Make It Pay Off

Rivalry between siblings is natural. It goes back to Cain and Abel. But rivalry does not have to be counterproductive. If the children aren't competitive, other employees may feel that they're "getting a free ride"...that they're not "pulling their own weight."

A child who is competitive tends to offset such feelings. Again, you must monitor the competition to be sure that it's fair.

Don't "take sides."

Don't give all of the choice assignments to your children.

Don't let your children take credit for someone else's achievements.

Don't give your children privileged information, extra advantages, special "tools" that will give them an unfair advantage over the others.

If They Succeed, You Succeed

Always be sure that your children are competing for worthwhile objectives—more sales, higher quality, less waste, greater profitability, new customers. Petty competition leads to petty bickering, and petty results. Strong competition leads to growth, to people who take pride in their accomplishments, to fostering a desire to climb to new and greater heights.

Chapter 6 Checkup

Children and the Family Business

After each of the following questions, indicate whether you agree or disagree. Our answers follow.

	Agree	Disagree
1. When brought into a family business, the children should be assigned to jobs that enable them to learn the business through observation, but prevent them from "getting in the way" of other workers.	___	___
2. Until the children are assigned to specific functions within the company, it is best to let them act as "ambassadors at large," contributing whatever and wherever they can throughout the organization.	___	___
3. It is a good idea for children to work in some other company before they join the family business.	___	___

	Agree	Disagree
4. If children enter the family business, they must "earn their own stripes."	_____	_____
5. Family businesses are different. Their structure, the duties of the employees, and even the salaries should be handled differently than in other companies.	_____	_____

From Our Point of View

1. **Disagree.**   The best approach is to rotate the children through a variety of jobs within the company. In that way, they will learn all aspects of the business, and concurrently you will be able to determine the functions for which they are best suited.

2. **Disagree.**   Introducing the children to the family business is not a game. The role of each member of the family who is involved in the business should be *clearly defined*.

3. **Agree.**   By working elsewhere, the children will have an opportunity learn something about business *on their own* and to see *how other companies* work. When they do join the family business, they can be expected to bring that experience, a supply of new ideas, a network of valuable business contacts, and a number of other benefits acquired at the other company along with them.

4. **Agree.**   If they are to have the respect of their co-workers, they are going to have to *earn* it. At the same time, the parents must turn over enough authority to enable the children to do their work as it should be done. If the parents attempt to second guess every decision the children make, it will do nothing to build the children's confidence, but it will convince the other workers that the children hold their positions only because of *who they are* and not *what they know*.

5. **Disagree.**   There should be absolutely no difference in organization, responsibilities, or compensation in a family business than in any other. It is particularly important, in our opinion, that the salary structure remain consistent and competitive with those generally practiced throughout the industry. If children are underpaid by the family firm, they probably will be unhappy and turn in unsatisfactory performances; but if they are overpaid, they may lose their competitive edge, become locked into the family firm, and start to coast on the strength of their family relationships.

7

The Extended Family

No two families are alike. Like snowflakes and fingerprints, families develop a character distinctly their own. No two have exactly the same number of people, the same mix of ages and sexes, the same standards, goals, attitudes, or outlooks.

Nowhere is this more evident than in the extended family, where every generation changes in some degree from the generation that came before.

As each husband brings something into his marriage from the lifestyle of his parents, each wife brings something into the marriage from the lifestyle of her parents. Inevitably, each one retains the things about their parents' lifestyle that they like the most and rejects the things they like the least. The result is a blending of two parental lifestyles plus the individual contributions of the couple themselves.

A Thought to Remember

Thirteen million American businesses, including 168 of the Fortune 500, are family-controlled companies. That's between 95 and 98 percent of all United States businesses.

These companies produce half of our gross national product and are responsible for creating 60 percent of all new jobs.

When a new family unit is created from such a union, each child borrows something from the parents but, once again, *adds* something of its own, and those differences often are more striking than the similarities. And so the cycle regenerates itself.

All of these changes in lifestyle are further influenced by changes in our society—morally, intellectually, politically, economically, and even legally.

The Seeds of Conflict

When a family business involves the members of more than a single family unit, it is understandable that a great deal more potential for conflict will exist. Each individual sees things in a slightly different way, and each is sure that *his* way is the *right* way. Old family disputes often resurface. Interfamily jealousies develop. Family problems can intrude on the operation of the business, and business problems can divide the family.

These things are regrettable, but for the most part they are avoidable, given some thoughtful planning and preparation.

A Thought to Remember

When employees are assembled into a company, whether they are relatives or "outsiders," the owner has the principal responsibility for seeing that they get along and take care of the firm's business.

Money and power are the most frequent causes of turmoil. Often they go together; occasionally they do not.

Many Startups Result from Family Loans

A study has shown that 18 percent of all new business startups—that's nearly one out of every five—are financed by loans from people in the family. As a source of startup capital, only the founder's personal funds and loans from a bank are used more frequently.

The same study showed that:

- 6 percent of the time, the founder's parents take an active role in the business.
- 3 percent of the time, in-laws do.
- 8 percent of the time, siblings do.

In other words, the extended family is involved in a new business startup at least 17 percent of the time.

Of course, these figures deal solely with startups. The longer a company is in business and the larger it becomes, the greater the probability that members of the extended family will take an active role in it.

- Older generations will seek work to occupy their leisure time and to supplement their retirement income.
- Members of the peer generation will seek employment as a haven from other, less enjoyable (and perhaps less well paying, less rewarding, or less secure) occupations.
- Younger generations will look for summer employment or parttime work.
- Even close friends or friends of relatives may elect to become part of your "extended family."

_____ **FAMILY SUCCESS SCENARIO 50** _____

STEW LEONARD'S DAIRY STORE
Norwalk, Connecticut

Stew Leonard's Dairy Store is certainly one of the most unusual groceries in the world.

Leonard, the youngest of seven children, grew up in Norwalk, where his father ran a dairy. Four months after Leonard graduated from college, his father died. So Leonard took over the family business.

In 1968, he expanded the business by adding a grocery to the dairy. Financed by a mortgage on his house, money that he'd saved for his children's education, and a loan from the Small Business Administration, he created a store that is truly unique.

- Instead of the traditional aisles, a labyrinth takes customers past the store's entire inventory.
- There is a petting zoo for children.
- There are animated displays.
- Employees dress in cow costumes and pass out helium-filled balloons.
- Leonard's salad dressing is made by a friend and neighbor — Paul Newman. (Leonard was instrumental in helping Newman to launch his product on the national market.)
- Customers are encouraged to put their ideas into the store's suggestion box.
- Leonard publishes a magazine-styled newsletter called _Stew's News_.

The store has a million-dollar kitchen that produces 200 salads and hot entrees a day. A glassed-in milk processing plant enables customers to watch as 5 million half-gallon cartons of milk and 1.5

million half-gallon cartons of orange juice each year zip past the
windows at the rate of 150 cartons per minute.

Leonard's "extended family"?

The store employs 22 of Leonard's own relatives, and half of his
600 employees also have relatives who work there.

Some Statesmanship May Be Required

Dealing with a relative—or even with a friend—can be much less "precise" than when you are dealing with an outsider.

With outsiders, you generally can be more direct without running the
risk of hurting their feelings. When dealing with friends and relatives,
more tact may be required.

In a business, things tend to be more black and white than most of us are
accustomed to around the home. There is less room for gray areas, which
often tend to become subject to debate, misinterpretation, or confusion. At
work, therefore, avoid imprecision; say *exactly* what you mean. If there are
two ways to do a job, both perfectly acceptable, it is better to state your
preference and make it a standard than to have half of your people doing
the work one way and the other half doing it another.

With members of the family, you may overplay a relatively insignifi-
cant situation simply to underscore a more important lesson for which it
may serve as an example. At work, however, this method of instruction
most likely will be seen as making a mountain out of a mole hill or, if not
that, then uncertainty or indecision on your part. Once again, it is best
to avoid such situations by being as precise and specific as possible when
giving instructions to your associates.

Brothers: Are They *All* Like
Cain and Abel?

Literature has not treated brothers kindly. According to the Bible,
mankind's *first* pair of brothers, Cain and Abel, resulted in history's first
fratricide. In Roman mythology, Romulus killed his brother Remus after the two had founded the city of Rome. In *The Man in the Iron
Mask*, author Alexander Dumas has his hero imprisoned in a dreary
dungeon—by his own identical twin!

Of course, life does not always parallel literature, and there have been
numerous brothers throughout history who have gotten along fa-
mously. The Wright brothers come to mind, and, more recently, the
Kennedys of Massachusetts.

Bred from the same genes and raised in the same environment, brothers frequently share many interests and many ambitions. Certainly, they know each other's strengths and weaknesses as well as anyone possibly could. What better foundation upon which to build a family business relationship?

One conclusion is inescapable, however: History provides an excellent example. If brothers have gotten along well throughout childhood, there is no reason to assume that they will not continue to do so. But if they have *always demonstrated animosity toward each other*, then almost certainly they should *not* think about becoming business partners.

Let Rivalry Serve a Purpose

If there must be rivalry among siblings, this competitive urge should be put to good use by directing it toward common goals, as many siblings have done. This obviously makes more sense than to work at cross-purposes with each other.

Carlton Caldwell is a dentist, and his brother John is a physician and medical researcher. In 1979, the brothers formed Caldwell Laboratories, Inc. in Kennewick, Washington. The company's specialty is in medical electronics to measure various brain functions. Caldwell Laboratories has been profitable from the beginning, and sales have continually grown by about 40 percent a year.

A Thought to Remember

A sense of tradition helps to tie people together in a family business. Time then strengthens both the ties and the business.

Henry and Richard Bloch used to prepare financial statements for small businesses. Then, as a favor, they began to do their friends' income tax returns. Next, they began to run a newspaper ad offering to do individuals' tax returns for "$5 and up." Today, H&R Bloch is a publicly held company with 4,000 company-owned outlets and 4,900 franchised outlets, and it employs as many as 40,000 people.

Turn a Hobby into a Career

Even a common hobby can result in a new business venture between brothers. Robert and Richard Blau, two Long Island, New York, teenagers, put together a magic act and entertained at local parties. Over the next seven years, their Chez-Zam company added designers, choreographers, technicians, and more than 120 performers as it grew into a multimillion-dollar business.

Tom Monaghan got started on the road to riches almost accidentally—through his brother.

_____ **FAMILY SUCCESS SCENARIO 51** _____

DOMINO'S PIZZA
Ypsilanti, Michigan

Growing up in Jackson, Michigan, Tom Monaghan lived an impoverished youth. When he was seven, his father died. When he was in his teens, he went into a Catholic orphanage.

As he grew, Monaghan worked three part-time jobs in order to earn money for college, but he left college before finishing one semester in order to join the Marines.

In 1960, his brother James suggested that they buy a pizza parlor in Ypsilanti called Domi-Nick's. Monaghan invested all the money he had in the venture, but a year later, James decided that he would rather try some other career. Tom bought him out by trading his Volkswagen for James' share of the business.

Monaghan renamed his pizza store Domino's, and he opened two more stores on borrowed money during the next five years. By 1965, his sales had doubled.

In 1967, Monaghan sold his first franchise.

Today, there are 4,800 Domino's pizza stores in the United States and abroad, and an average of two more are opened every day. Monaghan's chain grosses some $2 billion a year.

Plan for the Long Term

The "partnership" between Tom Monaghan and his brother was rather short-lived, but most family businesses created by siblings are built on more long-range expectations.

_____ **FAMILY SUCCESS SCENARIO 52** _____

HARLYN PRODUCTS, INC.
Los Angeles, California

Like Monaghan, Harold Weisbrod grew up in a poor family. His father, like Monaghan's, died when he was young; and like Monaghan, he served a hitch in the Armed Forces, where he was wounded and lost three fingers on his right hand.

After World War II ended, Weisbrod, his brother, and two partners pooled their money to start a watch repair business in Los Angeles. Weisbrod invested $3,000.

Due to his war injury, Weisbrod was unable to repair watches, so he formed a wholesale costume jewelry division of the company. When Weisbrod and his brother later separated from the other two partners, the Weisbrods retained the costume jewelry business.

Eventually, Weisbrod and his brother also went their separate ways, but Harold continued to operate the company that the two brothers had started together. He began to manufacture his own line of gold rings; and in 1972, he took the company public.

Today, Harlyn Products has a 45,000 square foot plant in Los Angeles and smaller plants in Bangkok and Korea. Sales amount to some $25 million a year, and Harold Weisbrod's personal fortune is estimated at some $5 million.

Successes Together ... Successes Apart

Not all siblings find success together. Many prefer to go their separate ways, even though they continue to be supportive of each other.

Edward Brennan is chairman and CEO of Sears Roebuck & Co. in Chicago, while his younger brother Bernard is president and CEO of rival Montgomery Ward & Co. Both their father and their grandfather once worked for Sears.

A Thought to Remember

Those who create family businesses tend to be less volatile than other entrepreneurs. They generally are more committed to the long term.

Multinational conglomerate Schlumberger Ltd. of New York started out as a family business, and then went public in the 1950s. Still well represented on the board, various members of the family, like the Seydoux brothers, have subsequently ventured off on their own. Jerome Seydoux heads Chargeurs SA, an aviation, shipping, and industrial firm headquartered in Paris. Nicolas Seydoux leads Gaumont, the largest film production and distribution company in France. And Michel Seydoux heads his own $100 million film production and aviation company.

A rather unusual example of two successful brothers who sprang from a family business involves the sons of Jack Thorne, founder of Scionics Corp., which manufactures microfilm data systems and electronic components; founder of the Pittsburgh Seed Fund, a $10 million investment company; and a professor of entrepreneurship in the Graduate School of Industrial Administration at Carnegie Mellon University. Thorne urged his sons John and Richard *not* to enter the family businesses, a situation which he feels "creates internal problems and puts the child under immense pressure." Instead, he encouraged John to form Cadmatics, a firm that creates computer-aided software for design engineers, and Richard to establish Iconnex Corp., which produces mechanical computer-aided engineering software.

Sisters: as Competitive as Brothers

If literature has been unkind to a great many brothers over the centuries, there is evidence that it often treated sisters with only a little more kindliness. The Bible treats Rachel and Leah almost as poorly as it does Cain and Abel. Mythology tells us about Antigone and her opposite, Ismene. Shakespeare gave us the three sisters who wrought destruction while competing for the favor of their father, *King Lear*.

And yet, particularly with the increased opportunities that have become available to women in the past few decades, sisters have become— and undoubtedly will continue to be—worthy contenders in numerous family businesses.

_____ **FAMILY SUCCESS SCENARIO 53** _____

BIGANE PAVING CO.
Chicago, Illinois

Anne Wilson and Sheila Bigane, two of five Bigane sisters, both played an important role in the family business after they graduated from college. Anne, who had studied engineering, took over the firm's paving division, while Sheila, who had majored in business, managed the ship refueling branch.

Since childhood, the two had been competitive: Anne had been slim; Sheila, pudgy. Anne was the older girl; Sheila, three years younger. Anne was the smart one; Sheila, the more popular.

With their three other sisters, the girls engaged in the usual competition to see who could win more of their father's favor, get the best job, marry the best husband, buy the nicest house, wear the finest clothes.

In 1988, the sisters' father died, and they were left to run the 94-year-old family business. With that, any gaps that had existed in their relationship disappeared.

"After our father died," says Sheila, "we just looked at each other and said, 'We've only got each other now.'"

The family business is doing just fine.

Brothers and Sisters: Strength Plus Compassion

Sibling partnerships also include many successful brother-and-sister partnerships. At its best, this combination extracts the best qualities of each: a mixture of strength and compassion.

_____ **FAMILY SUCCESS SCENARIO 54** _____

GARDNER SPRING & WIRE CO.
Chicago, Illinois

There were five Gardner brothers. Two of them founded the Oklahoma Spring Co. in 1965. A sister, Katherine, later joined the business.

In 1967, a Chicago company that would become Gardner Spring & Wire Co. was purchased. Marshall Gardner asked his sister to head it.

Between 1967 and 1970, Katherine Gardner Skinner (now Magrini) increased the company's sales from $50,000 a year to $400,000 a year. The family sold their holdings to the Barnes Group, the world's largest manufacturer of springs, in 1968. Katherine stayed on. Ten years later, aided by a million-dollar bank loan, Katherine repurchased Gardner Spring from the Barnes Group.

Now the company is producing over $10 million a year in sales.

Whom Can You Ask for Help?

Another sister-brother combination that has built a highly successful business together is Steve and Crystal Ettridge.

Steve borrowed $20,000 to form Temps & Co., a temporary office help firm in the Washington, D.C. area. He quickly persuaded his sister, then studying in France on a Fulbright scholarship, to join the company and help him manage it.

By 1987, Temps & Co. was placing over 7,000 temporaries in offices throughout the area and maintained a staff of 96 people in its own headquarters.

In a Family Business, You Often Need an Ally

Children have a natural reluctance to dispute their parents. From infancy, they have been taught obedience. Signs of rebellion were quickly stifled.

But when children enter the family business, it is equally natural that they will (a) want the support of their parents to make changes when they feel they are needed, (b) want the authority to make those changes, and (c) want to feel like a "partner" in the management and operation of the firm.

Parents, on the other hand, tend to feel most comfortable doing things "the old-fashioned way"—using techniques that have proven to be effective and profitable in the past. They may recognize the inevitability of change, but they don't have to welcome it. They may even discourage it, whether openly or in private.

Parents sometimes realize that their business has "outgrown" them, that new technology has evolved, making their own education and training obsolete. It is hard to keep up with modern advances, manage a business, and create a family, all at the same time.

Defensively, many parents often take a stubborn, hard-nosed position about the business that their children find difficult to penetrate. On such occasions, the presence and support of an ally—particularly a brother or a sister who can both understand the family/business situation and help to resolve it—can be invaluable.

_____ FAMILY SUCCESS SCENARIO 55 _____

ARTKRAFT STRAUSS SIGN CORP.
New York, New York

The history of one company, Artkraft Strauss Sign Corp., reflects both the right and the wrong way to integrate one's children into a family business.

Artkraft was founded by Jacob Starr, a Ukrainian ironworker who arrived in the United States in 1902.

Neon lighting was a new technology then, invented in France, and Starr acquired the North American rights to it. Artkraft became the predominant producer of outdoor signs in New York City, erecting most of those for which Broadway and Times Square became so famous.

Starr knew his business and he respected his workers, but he was a tyrant toward his family, especially toward his son Mel.

By the time Starr died in 1976, the company had 75 employees and did $5 million a year in sales. Mel was then 58 years old and had been working in his father's company for 37 years. But his father's callousness had made him bitter, and he decided that, henceforth, Artkraft would be run *his* way.

"Mel's way" was flamboyant and sales-oriented. It didn't matter if the job was underbid as long as he got the order. He roamed Broadway looking for business dressed in plaid suits, gold chains, gaudy ties, and a toupee, and he enjoyed making sales in a nightclub and sealing them with a handshake.

Mel ignored his workers, ignored the increasing theft of equipment and supplies, and ignored the need to update his manufacturing facilities with new machinery and tools. His trucks grew old and fell into disrepair.

A Thought to Remember

Father—merchant; son—playboy; grandson—beggar.

Mexican maxim

Worst of all, Mel was as tyrannical as his father had been, and just as negligent of his children. Both Tama and Jonathon Starr worked in the company from time to time.

Tama served as a receptionist and wrote sales proposals as a teenager, but was denied a more meaningful job after she graduated from college. Instead, she supported herself as a writer, as a songwriter, and as the founder of a theatrical troupe.

Jonathon didn't go to college. Instead, he spent seven years in India and one year in Africa, learned printing and photography, and worked as a sound engineer and as a writer of computer software.

Jonathon returned to Artkraft in 1977, a year after his grandfather's death. Three years later, his father suffered a heart attack, and Jonathon was on hand to help out. But the following year, when he had recovered from his illness, Mel returned and immediately precipitated clashes with his son.

In 1982, Tama returned to the company. Jonathon went off for a rest. But more importantly, brother and sister formulated a secret plan regarding how they eventually would run the family business. Their grandfather hadn't done it; their father wasn't doing it. So it was up to them to create a plan of their own.

Mel died in 1988 at the age of 69. Within hours, Jonathon was on his way home. Tama took immediate steps to implement their "plan of succession."

Since Mel's death, Artkraft has been thoroughly restructured:

- Computer-aided design has been introduced.
- Computer-aided manufacturing is being used.
- An extensive employee training program has been implemented.

- Decisions now evolve from executive meetings rather than authoritarian fiat.
- Three companies have been acquired and integrated into the firm, along with their own additions to the management team.

Tama Starr is the current CEO of Artkraft, and Jonathon is the company's chief operating officer.
A new generation has taken over.

Grandparents: An Older and Wiser Generation?

If parents sometimes seem demanding of their children in their zeal to see that they are properly equipped to compete in the world of business, grandparents often can be even more so.

John Tyson, now vice president of sales and marketing at Tyson Foods Inc., once had to get up at 3:00 A.M. to haul chickens from growers' farms to the family's processing plant.

August Busch III, now chairman and president of the giant Anheuser-Busch brewing company, once had to scrub beer vats.

Steve Marriott, grandson of J. W. Marriott, founder of the Marriott hotel chain, has cooked hamburgers in one of the company's Roy Rogers restaurants, worked in a test kitchen, manned the front desk in a hotel, and held a variety of catering, sales, and marketing positions in the company.

A Thought to Remember

For a family business to continue, one generation must be willing to let go, and another must be willing to take over.

Aunts and Uncles: Parents Once Removed

Sometimes an aunt or uncle is the one to provide a budding entrepreneur with the encouragement and training to launch a business.

In 1869, Charles Pillsbury persuaded his uncle John to lend him enough money to buy a one-third interest in a struggling Minneapolis flour mill. Within two years, young Pillsbury acquired complete control of the company, which he renamed C. A. Pillsbury Co. and developed into the world's largest milling empire. (The Pillsbury talents were not confined to business. Uncle John became Governor of Minnesota; nephew Charles served five terms in the Minnesota State Senate.)

Richard S. Reynolds joined his uncle's company, R. J. Reynolds Tobacco Co., in 1903. In 1912, the younger Reynolds struck off on his own; and in 1919, founded the U.S. Foil Co., which produced lead and tin foil for wrapping cigarettes (manufactured primarily by his uncle). By the mid-1920s, lead and tin foil was replaced by a new aluminum foil; and in 1947, Reynolds introduced the highly successful aluminum kitchen product, Reynolds Wrap.

Upon the retirement of Clyde Cessna in 1936, his nephew Dwane Wallace became president of Cessna Aircraft. During his 35 years as head of the firm, Wallace built Cessna into America's largest producer of small aircraft.

_____ **FAMILY SUCCESS SCENARIO 56** _____

FRIEDA'S FINEST/PRODUCE SPECIALTIES, INC.
Los Angeles, California

Frieda Caplan's aunt and uncle, managers of LA's Guimarra Brothers Fruit Co., taught her the produce business. Then, aided by a $10,000 loan from her father, Caplan started her own business selling exotic fruits and vegetables.

By 1977, Caplan's sales had reached $3.5 million a year, $5.5 million by 1978, and $11 million by 1985.

In-Laws: When the Chemistry Works, It Works

In-laws can also be very supportive of new business ventures. Two brothers-in-law, Burton Baskin and Irvine Robbins (Baskin was married to Robbins' sister), teamed up to create Baskin-Robbins Ice Cream in 1947.

_____ **FAMILY SUCCESS SCENARIO 57** _____

MONDO INVESTMENTS
Tucson, Arizona

In Arizona, the four Mondo sisters and their respective husbands have formed an ever expanding business alliance that has reached multimillion-dollar proportions.

Helen Mondo married Jim Robinson. Jean Mondo married Ray Dad. Twins Carolyn and Kathryn Mondo married Harlo Thorley and Don Baxla, respectively.

In the years that followed, Jim Robinson and Don Baxla became food distributors. Jean Dad became an elementary school teacher, and her husband Ray became a principal. Harlo Thorley became a construction foreman.

Then the family decided to try its collective fortunes in business.

Forming Mondo Investments, the four families began to buy and sell Arizona real estate. In 1982, when representatives of Peter Piper Pizza contacted the firm about a piece of property, the Mondo families liked what they were hearing about the Peter Piper franchise plan. A year later, the family opened a pizza franchise in Phoenix.

A year after that, the families opened three Peter Piper pizza parlors in Las Vegas, and two years later they paid $25,000 apiece to acquire eight Peter Piper locations in Tucson.

Now headquartered in Tucson, the families share the company workload. Don Baxla serves as the CEO, while his wife Kathryn handles the firm's advertising. Harlo Thorley and Jim Robinson handle construction and the remodeling of facilities, while Jean Dad is the office manager and head of special projects. Helen Robinson works in the office and supervises the personnel.

The families' families are now involved in the business as well. Helen and Jim Robinson have three children, one of whom works in the corporate office. Jean and Ray Dad have a married daughter who works in the business. Carolyn and Harlo Thorley have four children, including one who manages the Phoenix branch and another who works in a Tucson outlet. Kathryn and Don Baxla also have four children, including a daughter who works in the corporate office and a son who is supervisor of the Tucson branches.

"All four families have their money in dough," says Carolyn Thorley, with tongue in cheek. "Pizza dough."

The Extended Family Is Always Changing

Thus far, we have discussed many of the positive aspects of starting and/or managing a family business that involves individuals from outside the immediate family unit, i.e., the many types of people who constitute one's extended family. As part of this group, we have referred to grandparents, parents, aunts and uncles, adult siblings, nieces and nephews, cousins, in-laws, and even close friends who have earned the distinction of being considered "adopted" members of the family. Each of these has been immensely supportive, on occasion, to someone who is starting or operating a business.

We should add, however, that each of these family segments also has been nonsupportive, contentious, troublesome, and downright harmful on occasion.

Let the entrepreneur beware! If, as we have already demonstrated, a parent or a grandparent can be demanding of their sons and grandsons, should one demand any less of others? Is there any logical reason to go into business with someone who is less reliable, less skilled, or otherwise less capable of handling the business than a total stranger, simply because that individual is a relative? Family businesses do not succeed by providing employment for incompetents and malcontents. They succeed because the family is industrious, capable, dedicated, mutually supportive, and willing to channel its energies toward a common goal.

Families Do Not Come with a Guarantee

History has shown that family trees can produce many kinds of fruit—from geniuses to madmen. The notorious Cesare Borgia and his equally infamous sister Lucrezia were the children of a Pope, Alexander VI. Queen Elizabeth I had her cousin, Mary Stuart, Queen of Scots, beheaded.

This simply points out that family ties do not guarantee success, and that one should expect no less of a relative than of a total stranger. Such virtues as honesty, loyalty, and integrity are not restricted to one's relatives.

Family Loyalties Will Be Tested

As the owner of a family business, your loyalties will be tested many times. Be prepared for it. You will be required to be responsive, but reasonable ... forceful, yet tactful ... firm, but understanding. In most cases, you must be something of a judge, forced to determine how to comply with the requests of a friend or a relative without draining your own resources in the process.

You will get reasonable requests and unreasonable requests, and you will not be able to satisfy all of them. You may satisfy some and be able to compromise on others, but you will have to refuse a great many more.

Misguided Views of Success

Many people, unfortunately, have no idea how demanding it is to run a successful business. In their eyes, if you own a business, you must be rich. And if you are rich and are truly a good friend, you should be willing to help them out.

It will be up to you to educate them.

What kinds of things will be asked of you? Here are a few:

A job—full- or part-time

Free merchandise

Free services

The use of business equipment

A loan

Your guarantee of a bank loan

A discount

A job for some friend or relative

Donations to various organizations

Excessive credit, more favorable credit terms, or extensions on credit payments

A request to intercede with some other businessperson you may know regarding any of these issues

...and advice

The Sky Is the Limit—to Someone Else

For a true friend, no type of request seems to be beyond reason. I know of one instance in which the mother of a juvenile delinquent asked a friend to give her son a job and help straighten him out. She couldn't manage the boy, the schools couldn't manage the boy, the authorities couldn't manage the boy, but *she wanted her friend to do it*, and manage a business at the same time!

Jail a Relative? Let the Next Guy Do It

I know of another situation in which, at the urging of an uncle, a businessman employed a cousin whom he barely knew.

The businessman owned a restaurant, and he soon noticed that friends of his cousin were walking out without paying their bills. Then food began to disappear from the freezer and the storeroom. Next, the money in the till failed to match the totals on the cash register tapes.

After several unproductive conferences with his cousin, the businessman felt that there were only two avenues open to him—to have the young man arrested or to fire him. He let his cousin go.

But on his next job, the cousin was caught stealing and eventually was sent to jail.

To compound the irony, however, the compassionate restaurant owner who did not prosecute his cousin for being dishonest has not heard from either his uncle or the cousin since the young man left his firm.

Relatives or Strangers—Don't Relax Your Guard

If the moral of these stories is to exercise as much caution when you work with friends and relatives as any prudent businessperson would use when dealing with any other individual, then the lesson is well drawn. To be robbed by a relative or flim-flammed by a friend is a difficult and bitter experience. Consider the tragic experience of Julius Caesar, who was assassinated by a group of his closest friends.

Am I suggesting that a successful entrepreneur constantly needs to be distrustful, suspicious, paranoid? Certainly not. It simply bears pointing out that good judgment suggests exercising care in *all* your business dealings, regardless of their nature and regardless of who may be involved. The burden of concern necessarily falls on the one who has the most to lose, and where your business is concerned, that person is you.

Do They Belong in Your Company?

If you operate a family business, can you create safeguards and construct defenses to protect yourself from abuse *within your company* and yet maintain a "normal" relationship with your friends and family *on the outside?* Yes, if you think and plan ahead. Here are some recommendations:

If you elect to go into business with a partner:

1. *Be sure that you each view your goals, your ambitions, and your means of reaching them in the same way.* As the saying goes, "There are many ways to skin a cat."

Be sure that you and your associate(s) are going to work in tandem. Even if your partner is an outsider, from *your* perspective, you are forming a family business. Be careful who you let into the family.

If your prospective partners are members of the family, you should not assume that they think the same as you do. Be sure of it. Talk things out, in as much detail as possible.

Profit Pointer

Software is available—the People Compatibility Software System—that evaluates the strengths and weaknesses of any two people working together. If you would like more information on this software, contact me, Roger Fritz, at Organization Development Consultants, 500 Technology Drive, Naperville, Illinois 60563.

---

2. *Realistically assess what each of you will be bringing into the business.* Is it:

Money?
Specialized skills?
Business contacts?
Patents?
Equipment?
Real estate?
Technology?

Agree on what these things are worth and agree to apportion the profits (or the stock) accordingly.

3. *Define each person's responsibilities in detail.* In particular, agree on who is to be the boss. Set up a procedure for settling differences of opinion when they arise (and they *will* arise!).

4. *Determine in advance what is to happen if one of you wants to leave the business or when the first of you dies.*

Will the survivor have the right to acquire the other's share?
If a buyout is to take place, how is the value of each share to be determined?
If someone leaves the company, must he leave the essential assets behind or can he take them with him?
Will the person who leaves the company be allowed to go into competition with his former partner(s)?

5. *Put all considerations into writing.* Do not rely on your memory or the other party's memory. Memories are extremely fallible with the passage of time, especially when the parties separate under unfriendly circumstances.

The services of a good lawyer can be extremely helpful at this point.

6. *Be extremely sensitive to differences of opinion that arise during these discussions.* These are the points on which future conflicts are most likely to occur.

Compromise, but do not submit on any point that is of great importance to you. Do not be so anxious to get your business launched that you agree to something that you will regret later on.

If you are hiring an employee:

1. *Always keep in mind that the employee is entering your family business.* Family holds a somewhat different position, both inside the company and out, than somebody else — even somebody who may have been a close, long-time friend.

2. *Find out whether he or she — relative or otherwise — has the skills to do the job.* If the candidate claims prior experience, check it out with the previous employer. If the candidates do not have prior experience, be prepared to train them.

3. *Be sure that the candidate wants the job (I am tempted to say "needs" the job).* If not, the candidate probably will not be an eager, enthusiastic worker.

4. *For more than an entry-level position, check to see if any of your present employees has the qualifications for the job and deserves a promotion.*

5. *Ask yourself if the candidate seems willing to stay on the job for the long haul or is merely looking for a stopgap.* You don't want to be screening and training new employees constantly.

6. *Ask yourself if the candidate has the potential to assume greater responsibilities and move up in the organization.* You don't want people who have topped out because they probably will be lethargic and lacking in motivation.

7. *Determine whether the candidate is coming to you with any "strings" attached (not an uncommon condition when relatives are involved).* You must be free to pay, to promote, to reprimand, and to fire your employees according to the merits of their work, not because you "owe" it to them or to one of your friends or relatives.

If you are bringing relatives into the business:

1. *Let them know that they are coming into the business on a trial basis.* They are subject to the same standards of performance as everyone else.

2. *Show them no favoritism.* Nepotism can cause a great deal of dissention among the other employees, and make it a lot harder for your relative to gain acceptance from them.

3. *Treat them as fairly as you expect them to treat you.* Do not pay them less or work them longer hours than you would anyone else. Relatives are not slave labor.

4. *Restrict your socializing to after-work hours.* Don't use the business day to catch up on family gossip.

5. *Do not "cold shoulder" them on the job in the misguided belief that you are showing others that you "don't play favorites."* Other employees will know of your relationship and will misinterpret your behavior.

Chapter 7 Checkup

Anticipation Is the Key

1. How would you summarize the key reasons for the success of family businesses? Their failure?

2. On what basis should relatives be chosen to become involved in the family business?

3. How should the contribution of relatives be tested?

8

When the Family Grows Up or Breaks Up

Things would be so much easier if conditions remained stable. Unfortunately, nearly everything in life is in a constant state of flux, and one of life's most persistent challenges is learning how to deal with it.

Whenever a problem is solved, another one comes along to fill the void. We move through life from problem to solution and from problem to solution, a never ending process.

Part of the Aging Process

An added dimension to running a family business is the fact that families tend to grow up and break up. Everyone grows older, more independent, more opinionated, more competent—in short, passes through that perpetual state of change that is so common and yet so difficult to deal with.

If it is difficult to deal with the loss of a parent, it is even more so when that parent has been your mentor, your teacher, your confidant, your friend, and your business partner. If it is difficult to lose a key employee, it is even more so when that employee is your son or daughter. Yet each of these is an element of life's evolutionary cycle: changes that are to be expected, confronted, and dealt with in the normal course of events.

Planning Is the Key

Managing these situations successfully depends to a great extent on preparation. People *know* that the unexpected will—or at least can—occur, so they need to plan accordingly.

People often hate to think about the unexpected, much of which can be unpleasant. Some even ignore it until it occurs, by which time a crisis may have been created that will leave deep emotional scars on everyone involved.

By thinking and planning ahead, however, it is possible to remove (or at least reduce) the urgency of most situations, and all parties can then feel relieved with the knowledge that "Plan B" is ready and available for implementation.

Arrange for a Happy Ending

It is comforting to think that all family business situations have happy endings. The family business sustains Mom, Pop, and the kids over a considerable number of years. Then Mom and Pop enjoy a comfortable retirement, turning the business over to their talented and capable children, who eventually build the company into a highly respected, highly profitable multibillion-dollar empire.

Unfortunately, such stories are rare. Take the case of Amerco, the family-held parent of U-Haul.

Learn from the Mistakes of Others

Amerco was founded by Leonard Shoen, who not only nurtured the equipment rental giant to national prominence but managed to produce a family of 12 children through four marriages. Over the years, 80 percent of Amerco's stock was distributed among various members of the Shoen family.

In 1986, when Leonard Shoen reached 70 years of age, he was forced by his children to retire. E. J. "Joe" Shoen took over as chairman and CEO, while Samuel Shoen retained his post as president.

Almost immediately, however, major differences arose between Joe and Samuel Shoen, and in mid-1987 Samuel resigned as president.

Matters continued to worsen, with various children lining up on opposing sides of the intrafamily dispute. Leonard Shoen tried unsuccessfully to regain control of the company. At the 1989 shareholders' meeting, four of Leonard's sons got into a spirited fist fight. When some of the children sought to restructure the company or sell it, Joe Shoen fought off the idea. When it was rumored that some Amerco executives friendly to Joe might buy a block of shares in the firm, the opposing faction went to court to block the sale.

Fortunately, the Shoen family feud has failed to affect Amerco's operations so far. Revenues have risen to nearly $900 million and net income has nearly doubled—while the squabbling rumbles on.

The critical factor is to *plan ahead* in an attempt to forestall such unpleasant and potentially damaging situations.

Ask the "What If" Questions

Constantly ask yourself the following questions, and attempt to be totally honest and objective in reaching your answers. Then make your plans based on the future as *you envision it*.

Spouses

What if my spouse gets disabled and can't work?

What if my spouse decides to leave the company and go into another line of work?

What if there should be a divorce?

What if my health—or my spouse's health—turns bad?

Are my spouse and I agreed on when and how we will retire?

Are my spouse and I in agreement on how to dispose of the business when we either retire or die?

Parent/Owners

What should I do when my children go to college? Get married? Go into some other line of work?

Am I sure that the children *want* to take over the family business?

Am I sure that the children are *capable* of taking over the family business?

Without the income from the business, will I be able to retire comfortably?

Children:

What if Mom and Dad retire and I am left alone to run the business?

What if Mom and Dad were to die suddenly?

What if Mom and Dad sell the business?

Do I really *want* to make a career of this business?

Does the family business *satisfy* me as a career?

Is there sufficient growth potential in this business to last another generation?

Building a successful business can exact a regrettable toll on the founder's home life. Deprived of a great deal of parental companionship themselves, the offspring—regardless of their feelings toward the business—often elect to live their lives differently, even when it means going into another line of work.

Often, parents take it for granted that their children will learn the business, help to run it for a time, and then take over some day. Such presumptions have led to a great many disappointments, both for the parents and for the children.

Poor health, boredom, burnout, or the lure of a new challenge can cause sudden changes in a family's plans.

The Consequences of Divorce

Divorce is a factor that should not be overlooked. According to statistics, there will be one divorce for every two marriages through the immediate future. No one plans for things to work out that way, but they do, unfortunately.

One day your spouse is your principal business partner, your advisor, your confidant, and your staunchest ally. A few years later you are working with a pair of lawyers to determine how to divide your assets.

Some divorces are handled in a mature, amicable fashion; most are not.

When Will and Anne Ackerman divorced, they decided to remain partners in their business, Windham Hill Productions, Inc. of Palo Alto, California. Anne has since remarried, but remains active in the business. Unfortunately, such compatibility is rare.

Duane Meulners feared that California's community property law would cost him the control of his $10 million Dymek Corp. if he divorced his wife Kathleen. So he sought a hit man to get Kathleen out of the way. The hit man turned out to be an undercover San Jose police officer, and Meulners was convicted of solicitation to murder.

Arizona, Arkansas, Idaho, Louisiana, Nevada, New Mexico, Texas, and Washington are community property states as well as California. Other states are leaning in a similar direction regarding the manner in which family assets are to be divided following a divorce.

It is a good idea to have a thorough understanding of the law in your state.

Take Nothing for Granted

Rather than plan on things that they expect — or hope — or wish — will happen, wise business people plan from one probable event to the next. They anticipate the unexpected. They monitor their plans along the way, constantly making sure that events are taking place as expected, but always prepared to make changes if they are necessary.

Rather than *presume* their childrens' wishes for the future, they talk to the children, often and openly. They determine what the childrens' interests and ambitions are. Their questions ask *if*, rather than *when*.

This concept warrants further exploration.

One parent may ask: "What responsibilities can I turn over to Lisa *when* she enters the business?" A wiser parent will ask: "What responsibilities can I turn over to Lisa *if* she enters the business?" Having considered that question, the wise parent will reach a decision. That decision is then discussed with Lisa to determine if she will be happy in the role that her parents envision for her. If she won't, the parents had better rethink the situation.

One Question at a Time

If there are important responsibilities to be delegated, and Lisa doesn't want to handle them, who will?

If Lisa wants to handle responsibilities for which she doesn't have the experience, training, or aptitude, perhaps this is the time to see that she gets that experience or training, or to convince Lisa to go into something for which she has greater aptitude.

If Lisa doesn't want to fill the role that her parents have envisioned for her, perhaps what she is *really* trying to tell her parents is that she's not interested in being a part of the family business at all. That she would rather do something else with her life. The daughter of one of my current clients wants to be an actress, for example, and has struggled for several years over how to break the news to her father without "breaking his heart."

People who would not think of trying to squeeze a size 10 foot into a size 8 shoe often take the misguided view that they can squeeze their children into careers that simply do not "fit" them. The consequences generally are disastrous. In our view, children should never be admitted to the family business unless they want to be involved in the family business.

Leave Enough Room to Change Your Mind

Let's get back to the matter of considering *if*, rather than *when*, as you plan for the future.

The word *if* recognizes the possibility that unforeseen changes will occur between the time a plan is formulated and the time it can be executed.

When presumes that nothing unforeseen will happen, that no changes can occur, and that coming events will transpire just as you have predicted they would. *When* also forecloses the possibility of making timely adjustments within your plan in case some expected event does *not* occur.

Let's look at an example.

You decide to expand the office *when* sales reach $2 million a year. All available data indicates that you will reach the $2 million figure by the end of the year, so you engage an architect, let a building contract, and begin to hire some additional personnel.

Then the unexpected occurs. A major competitor goes out of business. Instead of hitting $2 million, your sales zoom to $5 million. The expansion that you had planned for is no longer adequate, and the number and mix of personnel that you have hired has to be altered drastically. All of your previous plans have now gone "out the window."

This is a happy scenario. With a nice increase in business, you certainly will be able to offset the change in plans somehow. But what if the situation were reversed?

If the Shoe Were on the Other Foot...

What if instead of going out of business, your competitor expands or introduces a new product line? Instead of increasing, your sales drop. All your available resources must now be focused on meeting this new and unexpected challenge. Expansion is out of the question. Survival is paramount.

The point is that nobody knows what the future may bring. It is important to plan, but planning should be predicated on what you will do *if* something occurs as well as *when* it occurs.

Getting too far ahead of one's self can be dangerous; and trying to "shoe-horn" your circumstances into situations where they simply do not fit can be disastrous.

Leave an Escape Route

Plan, but plan cautiously. Allow every possibility that some changes will occur, and factor a few "escape routes" into your plan. Try not to paint yourself into a corner.

The same concept applies to dealing with family situations in the business. Anticipate what may happen, but do not assume something to be a fact until it is indeed a fact.

What sort of situations are we speaking of?

Clarify Your Assumptions

Let's assume, by way of illustration, that you are working in your parents' business, along with a brother and a sister. Let's assume that your parents are in their early sixties, that you and your siblings are married, that each of you has children of your own, and that the business is reasonably healthy and profitable (that is, there are no immediate business crises to be concerned about).

What sort of "family situations" could one anticipate from circumstances of that sort? First, of course, there are the interests and welfare of your parents to be considered.

Do your parents plan to retire in the near future?

If so, who will take charge of the business?

Will your parents be taking profits from the company to support their retirement?

Will they want to sell the company to support their retirement?

Has the family fully discussed these points?

Is everyone in full agreement with the plans that have been made?

Break Your Plan into Smaller Pieces

Let's explore some of these questions in greater depth.

Whether or not a specific date has been set, your parents should be thinking about retirement, having reached their early sixties. They also should be conscious of their own mortality. If your father were to pass away suddenly, for example:

Would your mother be able to operate the business alone or with your help?

Would the business have to be sold to meet expenses?

Has any plan been discussed to cover these possibilities?

Has a successor been chosen to run the business after your parents retire?

Has the successor been properly trained for the job?

Is everyone satisfied with the selection, and assured that the successor can handle the task?

If any of these questions has not been addressed, now is the time to resolve differences. Don't wait until there is a crisis.

Consider All the Options

If there is any question about succession or about the possibility of having to sell the business, perhaps it is time to think about a buyout. The siblings might agree to purchase the company from their parents for a specified sum and over a mutually agreeable time span. This arrangement assures the parents of a specific income, and it permits the children an opportunity to plan their own futures more precisely.

Perhaps other people, such as other relatives or valued long-term employees, should be included in the buyout proposal. The sooner such details are considered and decided on, the better it will be for everyone, and the smoother the eventual transition will be.

If your parents have sufficient means to bequeath the business to their children, rather than sell it to them, they may find that there are a number of advantages to doing so while they are still alive rather than waiting to make the transfer through their wills. Such transfers need not be executed all at once and can be made in increments over a period of years, if that would be more desirable. Be sure to analyze the tax situation very carefully to be sure that the heirs are the beneficiaries of the transfer and not the government.

One More Advantage to Incorporation

At a time like this, having the company incorporated will prove to be a considerable advantage. It generally is far easier to sell, give away, or bequeath shares of stock than it is to divide less tangible assets or to apportion those assets to people according to some complicated mathematical formula.

Whatever the decision, it is highly advisable to make it well in advance. Few things are as frustrating as having to go through the courts to settle the estate of an individual who has left no will.

Other family situations can arise as well and should be anticipated. Do you have a good relationship with your siblings? Do your respective families get along?

Some other things to consider are your siblings' respective levels of training and experience, their other responsibilities within the company, their relationships with your parents, and your own personal and individual interests and ambitions.

Who Will Take Over?

One point cannot be stressed too strongly: Once your parents leave the company, *someone must be in charge*. Even if all of the children hold equal shares in the business, one must have the authority to run it. It should not be necessary to poll the entire family before a decision can be reached.

Committee decisions are seldom the best. They are just a consensus, and a consensus is like an average. Everyone knows how averages work: One person scores 100 percent on a test, another scores 60, and the average is 80. Who should be running your company—the one who scores 100, the one who scores 60, or the one who scores the average? 100, the one who scores 60, or the one who scores the average?

A number of years ago, a friend of mine phrased it beautifully when he said: "The average person can be looked at in two ways—he's either the best of the worst or the worst of the best." There is no distinction in being average.

Compensating a Leader Fairly

If one of you is going to have the responsibility of leading the company, shouldn't he or she get a greater share of the profits?

How do you propose to resolve that? Perhaps the siblings who shoulder less of the business responsibility will agree to let the business leader draw a larger salary. Perhaps they will agree to sell the business leader a few of their shares in the company as compensation for the extra work. Perhaps some kind of a bonus plan can be developed.

Whatever the choice, this is another of those "foreseeable" family situations that should be addressed long before a major crisis occurs.

Who's in and Who's out?

Another potential problem exists: Once Mom and Dad are no longer involved in the business, perhaps one or more of the siblings will want out as well. If everyone wants out, the family can simply sell the company and divide the proceeds.

But what if one wants out and the others want to continue with the business? In some cases, the departing owner sibling(s) will be willing and able to leave their assets in the company as an investment. In other cases, they may want to withdraw their assets for other purposes, possibly causing a significant financial problem for those who choose to continue with the business.

Perhaps the remaining owners will be in a position to buy out the departing sibling(s). Perhaps the company itself will have sufficient funds to cover the purchase of the departing sibling's share. In either case, a sale price will have to be established and the terms of the buyout negotiated. A bank loan may be required—or even a new partner.

Once again, the ability to deal in the shares of an incorporated firm will make such negotiations a great deal easier to manage.

Let the Others Know How You Feel

Obviously, the more open dialogue there is among the siblings, the more frank discussion there is about their individual plans and intentions, and the more advance warning one sibling gives another before doing something that will affect the entire business, the easier it will be for everyone concerned to work out a plan that will be the most rewarding for all.

Major family crises can critically affect the operation of a business. If the owners' concentration is directed elsewhere, the business can suffer—a situation that benefits no one. If critical assets are suddenly withdrawn, redirected, or tied up for an extended period of time, the business also will suffer.

Once again, the value of advance planning and anticipating the "what if" situations is obvious.

What About the Extended Family?

So far, we have explored some of the concerns of the retiring parents in our hypothetical web of predictable family situations. We also have analyzed some of the concerns of the eventual sibling heirs. But there is still another facet to be considered: the concerns of the later generations and other elements of the extended family. They, too, are involved in the fortunes of the family business and are deserving of consideration.

Many of these younger people may already be directly involved in the business. Some may be in college, preparing themselves to take a place in the business. Others may be following pursuits of their own and could care less.

Each of these is a factor to be dealt with, however. To some extent, we have discussed situations involving children in Chapter 6 and situations involving the extended family in Chapter 7, but much of that discussion was based upon the viewpoint of the first- or second-generation businessperson—the one in the best position to call the shots.

Here we are thinking about circumstances in which later generations of others within the extended family might have to handle business situations without the advantage of absolute authority. We are talking about issues that are much less related to the "what if" of succession once the founders retire, die, or decide to sell, but with the thorny day-to-day situations that often occur on the job.

A Question of Apples and Oranges

How do these situations differ? We couldn't begin to illustrate every possibility, but we can cite a few possibilities that may be worth thinking about:

- *Suppose your son has just received a college degree in business and your sister's daughter has had four years of experience on the job.*

  Which one deserves a higher position in the company?
  How do you and your sister resolve that question?
  How does your son resolve it with his cousin?

- *Suppose your brother and sister feel that your son is drawing too much salary and want you to demote him.*

  What do you do?

- *Suppose you are in charge of the company's manufacturing operations and your niece is in charge of marketing. You disagree on a major, and perhaps costly, issue. You are one-third owner of the company, but your niece's parent (also a one-third owner) sides with her on the issue.*

  How do you resolve this situation?

- *Suppose you feel that one of your nephews is not pulling his weight in the company and should be fired.*

  What should you do?

- *Suppose your sister feels that another employee is more deserving of a promotion than your daughter.*

  How do you handle the situation?

I'm sure that the nature of these problems is apparent by now.

When you are in absolute control, you can do pretty much what you please. When you are a third- or fourth-generation heir and hold a minority position in a family-held business, you don't enjoy that luxury.

Indeed, as a minority owner you discover that you must function very much as you would if you were working for General Electric or some other large corporation, rather than a family business.

Put the Company First in Most Cases

Any business decision that is to be workable in situations such as those just described — and also be acceptable to your co-owners — will have to be made solely on its merit, *without regard to the relationships involved.*

Easier said than done? Remember this incontrovertible fact: Bad decisions hurt the company, hurt you, hurt your brother and sister, hurt your children, and ultimately hurt their children as well. Being passed over for a promotion, being demoted on the job, losing out in an argument, or even being fired may result in some temporary embarrassment for those involved. But since you are all members of a family — and therefore the beneficiaries of a sound, profitable business — whatever benefits the company will benefit each of you.

Look at the Dollars and Cents

Some figures might explain how this works: Let's say that you have a $5 million company that is producing a profit of 10 percent, or $500,000, a year. Your third of the firm is worth some $166,667 a year in income.

Now suppose that your niece, the head of marketing, convinces you to follow her advice and, as a result, sales increase 50 percent with no reduction in profit margins. You now are part owner of a $7.5 million company producing $750,000 in profit a year. Your share jumps in value to $250,000 a year.

Your company has prospered, you have prospered, and you also now know that the company's marketing is in the competent hands of a very smart cookie — your niece.

Even the "Little Fellow" Benefits

Sure, you say, but in this case you're "the old man" — a one-third partner. What about the young nephew who has been fired for not doing his job? Is he supposed to see it the same way?

Let's take a look: In the same $5 million company, replacing the lackluster nephew with a more capable person makes it possible to increase the profit margin from 10 percent a year to 15 percent a year — from $500,000 in profit to $750,000 in profit.

If, like you, the nephew is one of three children and if, like you, he has fallen heir to one-third of his parent's share of the company, then one-ninth (one-third of one-third) of the profit "belongs" to him. Instead of a share worth some $55,000 a year in profit, his share increases in value to over $82,000 a year. He's lost his job, but he's received a "bonus" of some $27,000 *per year*! Meanwhile, he's free to look for another job, maybe one that he will like better.

So you see, it isn't a matter of responding to personalities or relationships, but one of doing what's best for the company that matters. If the company prospers, everyone benefits; if it fails, everyone loses.

Success and prosperity can smooth a lot of ruffled feathers and wounded egos.

How to Handle Bad News

Obviously, there are going to be some disputes. And in every dispute, you can expect that there will be a winner and a loser.

The difficult part is that of "breaking the news" to the loser and getting that person to accept it. If you can do that, business can proceed smoothly; if you can't, you can expect the loser to do a great deal of carping (at best) and possibly submit a resignation (at worst). This unpleasant task is made even more so when the individual with whom you are dealing is a member of the family.

You can do a few things to make the job easier:

Let the individual know that his suggestion was carefully considered and that it wasn't rejected offhand. Nothing aggravates people more than to think that their ideas aren't taken seriously.

Let the individual know that there was merit in his point of view, but that, on balance, it was felt that the other approach would work out better.

If you can identify any advantages, show the individual *how he or she will benefit* from your decision. It's a lot easier to accept another person's point of view if you can see that there's some value in it to you.

Time Can Be a Valuable Ally

Don't be hasty in making tough decisions unless you have to. Take some time.

Before demoting someone or firing employees, for example, give them some advance warning. Let them know what's expected of them and where they are falling short. Give them an opportunity to meet your standard. If they do, you may not have to get unpleasant; if they don't, they will know why you are taking the action that you are.

Set the Standards Beforehand

In a similar manner, it will be much easier to explain to people why they are being passed over for promotion if you have previously announced the qualifications for the job and the criteria used in selecting the one who will get it.

As disappointed as a person may be when they do not get a promotion, they will understand that your decision had nothing to do with them personally or with your relationship. They will treasure their next promotion all the more.

Show Some Flexibility When You Can

Whenever possible, *arbitrate* the tough decisions. Don't make all of the tough calls yourself. Get others to share in the process. That way, you're not only getting the best input and advice on the situation, but you are sharing the responsibility.

Sure, someone has to be responsible for making the final decision, but you may find that that decision is not as one-sided or as unpopular as you may have thought.

Certainly, everyone should be made aware of the facts and the reasons for doing what has to be done.

You Can't Avoid *All* the Tough Calls

When it comes to announcing bad news, my general feeling is that bad news should come from the boss or at least from someone in the direct chain of command.

In family businesses, however, chains of command are often somewhat obscured, and the interpersonal relationships of the individuals might justify a greater measure of flexibility. In some families, the best person to convey bad news may be a parent. In others, it may be a favorite aunt or uncle, brother or sister, grandparent, cousin, or even some unrelated third party, such as a close friend. Nobody likes to disappoint their own children. Yet who understands a child better than a parent, and who is in a better position to handle the job more tactfully? Suffice it to say, each situation merits its own method of treatment.

The main objective is to convey bad news in the smoothest, kindest, and least disruptive way possible. A strong secondary objective is to do it in such a way as to conclude the matter and not let frustrations escalate beyond proportion and into other matters unrelated to the issue at hand.

Everyone Meets Some Disappointment in Life

We must realize that the wishes of our children are often different from ours, that their interests are different, that their ambitions are different, and that their skills are different. No matter how much we may wish it otherwise, not all our children will want to follow in our footsteps. Frankly, not all of them would succeed if they tried.

It is pathetic to watch parents try to make children conform to some lifestyle that the parents have preconceived for them. It is even more pathetic to watch children struggle to satisfy their parents' preconceptions (or to be constantly rebelling against them), forever concerned that somehow, no matter how hard they try, they will never "measure up" to their parents' expectations. Many parents are never satisfied with anything less than their hopes that they have envisioned for their children, and the children are rarely happy living a life that is of someone else's design.

It is my belief that parents should encourage their children to pursue their own interests and automatically assume that those interests will be different than theirs. If—lo and behold—the children show an interest in the family business, *then* take steps to see that they become involved. In this way, the parents are less likely to be disappointed, and the children, free to follow their own inclinations and make their own decisions, will be under far less pressure.

When children do decide to enter the family business, both they and their parents should realize that it is because the children *want* to participate and not because they were coerced into it or because they are simply trying to please their family.

Parents Often Need to *Listen* More and *Talk* Less

Frequent and open dialogue between parents and their children provides the best barometer. In such conversations, the parents should concentrate on *listening*, not talking; and they should take pains to be sure that they are hearing *what their children are trying to say*, not listening solely to hear what they want to hear.

If there are several children in the family, it is highly unlikely that they all will want to work in the family business. Those who do not should not be made to feel inferior to those who do. Those who do not should not be deprived of the family's support when they follow some other pursuit.

**There Are Things That *Can't*
Happen, But *Do***

Be prepared for surprises. Often, parents who had thought that they
would turn the family business over to their son one day have eventually
turned it over to a daughter instead. Parents who have had high hopes
for their oldest child have frequently discovered that their youngest
showed the greatest potential.

Spouses often play a key role too.

_____ **FAMILY SUCCESS SCENARIO 58** _____

McKENNA INDUSTRIES
Troy, Michigan

In 1952, Patrick McKenna founded McKenna Industries. A year
later, he was killed in an automobile accident, leaving his wife
(Helen), a 14-year-old daughter, and an 8-year-old son.

McKenna Industries, which makes production models for the
automobile, aircraft, and aerospace industries, had five employees
at the time.

Helen McKenna took over the family business.

By 1988, she expanded the firm to include five companies with
150 employees and $11 million a year in sales. Her son Mike is
now president of the company and "Mom" serves as chairman of
the board.

**Take Assistance from Every
Possible Source**

Others, such as a son- or daughter-in-law, may join the family firm and
prove to be valuable contributors to its success.

_____ **FAMILY SUCCESS SCENARIO 59** _____

RAM GOLF CORP.
Melrose Park, Illinois

Ram Golf Corp. is run by three brothers: Jim, the president; Lyle,
head of research and development; and Al, who is head of marketing.

Also on the management team, however, are Jim's son Scott
(sales), Lyle's son Tom (apparel), and Al's son Gary (design), as
well as a brother-in-law Al Norby.

Adaptability Is the Key to Handling Change

All these examples offer ample proof that one should be neither too quick to form presumptions nor too slow to make alterations in the game plan whenever circumstances change. The best plans generally are predicated on the *if* and not the *when* of an equation.

As families grow up—and eventually begin to break up—one can anticipate having to cope with a many complicated problems. When some of those problems involve the business, they can be particularly difficult, but the trauma can be greatly reduced for those who remain flexible, who keep an open mind, who recognize the inevitability of change and the importance of responding to it quickly when it occurs. Those who are too rigid, too set on a predetermined plan, or too committed to the status quo to allow for the fine tuning of their lives when necessary—will be the ones who find those later years to be the most difficult.

Chapter 8 Checkup

An Exercise in Planning for the Unknown

List the ten worst things that you think could happen to your family business. (Ignore such obvious disasters as fire or other acts of God.)

1. _____
2. _____
3. _____
4. _____
5. _____
6. _____
7. _____
8. _____
9. _____
10. _____

For each item just listed, write down what step(s) you have taken to minimize that threat to your company.

1. _____
2. _____
3. _____
4. _____
5. _____
6. _____
7. _____
8. _____
9. _____
10. _____

Are there any items on the first list that are left unprotected on the second list? What do you propose to do about them?

Are there any additional safeguards that you might take to protect any facet of your business?

9

When Somebody Wants Out

It almost goes without saying that people rarely go into a business thinking that it will fail, that they will become bored with it, that they will do anything less than give it their best shot, or that the day will come when they simply want out.

Certainly, every entrepreneur can envision the time to retire, to pass the business on to the children, to sell it to somebody else, or to take the company public. But all of these are planned and carefully orchestrated decisions, not unexpected bolts from the blue.

Few people these days have any thought of dying with their boots on. If their businesses are operating soundly, if their successors have been carefully selected and trained, if their retirements have been thoughtfully planned, then their eventual departures should cause no particular turmoil.

It is only when a key individual's departure is sudden, unannounced, unanticipated, and hence unplanned that problems arise. An unexpected drain on the company's reserves...a void in the operation that nobody is in a position to fill...the loss of key technology, critical customers, or suppliers...the possibility of having to contend with a new competitor who knows as much about your business as you do--all can be extremely traumatic.

Facing the Unexpected Once Again

Still, unexpected things do occur.

An illness in the family or a sudden financial reversal can make it necessary to change one's plans in midstream, no matter how well things may be going.

163

A prospective partner can have a change of heart.

Anticipated funding can fail to materialize.

Startup costs can be greater than expected.

Any one of these and similar unexpected problems can be devastating.

What can you do to protect yourself from these "unforeseeable" situations? And if one does occur, what can you do about it?

Start from the Start

Thorough advance planning is your best means of protection, of course. We have said this before—many times.

When you start a new business, calculate your startup costs carefully. Allow a little something extra for those unexpected increases in cost or to cover overlooked items. Be *sure* that the necessary financing is available. Get people's commitments, including those of a potential partner, in writing.

Until all of these factors are *assured,* do not enter into contracts involving leases, the purchase of materials or equipment, or the delivery of goods or services to potential customers.

If you enter into a lease for an office or a store, sign an agreement to buy equipment, or agree to purchase from certain suppliers—and then discover that you have to back out of the deal, it may cost you money.

If you agree to provide goods or services to a customer and then fail to meet that commitment, you may be sued and end up in court.

In short, it is wise to go into a business slowly and cautiously. There will be opportunities to move more aggressively once your company is firmly established.

Pick a Good Partner

There are a number of ways to forestall an eventual breakup with a potential business partner. From the outset:

1. Look for a partner whose strengths compensate for your weaknesses, and vice versa.

2. Look for a partner who likes to do the jobs that you do not, and vice versa.

3. Be sure your business philosophies are compatible. Are you both committed to the long term rather than the short term, for example? Will your business objective be high risk, high profit, or slow, steady growth and security?
4. Try to avoid getting in each other's way by setting up clearly defined areas of responsibility.
5. Try to avoid second-guessing each other's work.
6. Schedule regular meetings to discuss problems, evaluate your progress, and plan your next moves.

After the Startup

Predictably, a businessperson's problems do not end after a successful startup. The potential of a breakup always exists. Then what?

To begin with, do not frustrate yourself too much by trying to determine the reasons for your associate's departure. That is a decision individuals must make for themselves, and it is one that is seldom made casually.

If you know that your associate's departure is due to some minor difference of opinion, try to negotiate a workable solution, but don't offer—or expect—too much. Neither of you will be happy with an altered situation if it requires you to contradict any of your basic beliefs, and you probably will discover, more likely sooner than later, that your "band-aid" attempt at a solution will not work.

Try to Determine Why Your Partner Wants to Leave

Attempts to change your partners' minds generally will tend to:

Make them more defensive in their position.

Widen any differences that exist between you.

Draw out the eventual separation.

Trying to be understanding of your partners' decision will:

Tend to make them more conciliatory.

Enable you to calmly work out a mutually-acceptable plan for the separation.

Result in a quicker, smoother, and more amicable settlement.

In a sense, it's damned if you do, less damned if you don't.

Except when the separation is due to something like health or a severe financial situation, you can assume that it indicates there is something wrong in the business. Don't become defensive about it. Try to determine what the trouble is so that you can correct it before it causes additional problems.

Inside, Outside—Does It Matter?

The difficulties of going through a breakup are the same whether you are parting company with a relative or with a partner from outside the family. Each individual will be anxious to protect their own interests, and that should be your objective as well.

Whatever the circumstances—or who's "at fault"—a breakup nearly always involves tensions and pressures. Tempers often flare.

It is a time to demonstrate extraordinary patience and keep a cool head. Act—and react—cautiously. Think every situation through carefully. If you need outside advice—from a consultant, a banker, a lawyer, or an accountant—get it.

Surviving a Breakup

In the midst of such business adversities, it is critical to concentrate on positives, rather than negatives. Do not wallow in self-pity or cast about for somebody or something to blame for your situation.

Take a careful look at your assets. Write them down. Then review the list to see how you can mobilize those assets to help you overcome the problems before you.

Reduce Your Inventory

If you have excessive inventory, perhaps you can alleviate a short-term cash crunch by lowering your prices and having a sale to raise quick revenue.

Consider Sale-Leaseback

If you own your property—or some costly equipment—perhaps you can arrange a sale-leaseback agreement, which could bring in some needed cash. Under the terms of such an agreement, you sell your property (or equipment) to another party, who then leases it back to you. You get some immediate cash and your company continues its normal operations, even though your overhead may increase somewhat to cover the terms of the leaseback.

Get Warehousing Assistance

If you maintain a warehouse to store raw materials or finished goods, perhaps you can eliminate that extra overhead by getting your suppliers or your customers to inventory those items for you.

Use Sales Reps

If you are spending a lot to maintain a large marketing organization, perhaps you can consider doing business through a network of sales representatives.

Try Commercial Delivery Systems

If you are maintaining a costly fleet of delivery vehicles, perhaps you should consider the use of commercial carriers.

Giving a Little Can Get You a Lot

As you write down your list of assets—the things that you have going for you—it is more than likely that you will discover how those assets can be made to help you through your difficulties.

Dwelling on your problems rather than seeking potential solutions to those problems will only waste time, cause the problems to escalate and multiply, and ruin your disposition.

Concentrating on the positive aspects of your situation will help you to conquer whatever negative events may arise.

It's Not the Gross But the Net That Matters

When good times are at hand, it is not how much money you have or how much money you owe that matters, it is *how much money there is left after you have paid your bills*. In troubled times, the situation is the same. If you can make a list of your assets, deduct your debits, and *have something left over*, then you will do all right.

Temporary Difficulties vs. Long-Range Problems

When a key individual in the company wants out, it may create some temporary problems, but that is not to say that the long-term outlook is diminished. If you had a good idea going into business, it's still a good idea.

You may never have thought about having to run the company by yourself, but that's not to say that you can't do it. It's largely a matter of changing your outlook.

If you need some help, *hire it*.

The Situation May Not Be All Bad

Few individuals are indispensable. Indeed, I have found that most people have contributed about as much to a company as they are able to contribute after five years or so. After that, they tend to fall into a routine—to go about their work robotically—without making any additional major contributions.

Certainly, their familiarity with the business, their loyalty, and the contacts that such individuals establish over the years are valuable—but not irreplaceable.

Your Training Program Pays Off

If you have been hiring and training your employees properly, there should be people ready and able to take the place of those who are leaving. These employees have been working and waiting for their opportunity to advance. Give it to them.

Outsiders Can "Fill the Gaps"

If outsiders must be brought in, give them the same freedom and authority that you had vested in the ones they are replacing. Take advantage of their eagerness and enthusiasm. Give them the opportunity to introduce new ideas and different approaches to their work. They are new members of your team, not merely clones of their predecessors. Give them a chance to contribute whatever they have; don't try to make them be something that they are not.

Your attitude is extremely important when someone new is brought aboard. If you had a grudge against people who have now gone, don't inflict it upon the persons you have chosen to take their place.

> ### A Thought to Remember
>
> *Success depends on three things: who says it, what he says, how he says it; and of these three things, what he says is the least important.*
>
> —*John, Viscount Morley*

Comparisons are inevitable, I suppose, but always vocalize such comparisons in a positive manner. Instead of saying, "Dave was always at work 30 minutes earlier than you" (which really doesn't matter anyway), say things like, "Our orders have increased five percent since you joined us," or "I've noticed a great improvement in morale since you arrived."

Let new people know that they are welcome, that you have noted their accomplishments, and that those accomplishments are appreciated.

These matters are of particular importance if the new person has a financial interest in the firm. If, for example, someone new were to buy the interest of your previous partner, he or she may not be someone of your personal choosing, but it is important for you to integrate that person into the organization as smoothly and as quickly as possible.

Find time to hold candid, open discussions and to explore every aspect of the business with them, particularly any areas in which there may be problems.

Don't dump all of your problems on newcomers. Let them carry their share of the load, and be receptive to their recommendations for improvement, if any.

It's a Whole New Ballgame

Getting a new partner is like taking a new spouse. You are establishing a new relationship and starting with a fresh, clean slate.

Correct any shortcomings that you may have had in the past. Most of us have them, and frankly yours may have contributed to the loss of your previous partner.

Realize that you are now dealing with a totally different person, and demonstrate your appreciation for whatever contributions this new individual can bring to your relationship.

Keep Your Future Options Open

The breakup of a business partnership tends to prove the wisdom of an old adage, "Don't burn your bridges behind you."

Down the line, as unlikely as it may seem at the moment, you may want to form another partnership with those individuals, or approach them for advice, or ask them for a loan. You may need their recommendation to obtain financing from the bank. You may need the same business contacts, or want to serve the same customers, or buy from the same suppliers as your former partners. Intemperate behavior now might jeopardize one or all of those possibilities.

Do not let one business reversal destroy your financial or personal reputation. And above all, do not let it destroy your desire to have a successful business of your own.

It's Never Over Until You Quit

Above all, you should not accept failure too readily. Many entrepreneurs have failed on their first, second, or third efforts only to find success later on through persistence and determination.

Instead of "going down with the ship," do everything in your power to salvage something out of a situation that might at first seem hopeless. After all, you already have invested a great deal of thought, time, and energy in the project.

If you lose one partner, try to find another.

If you are strapped for money, see if you can't scale down your ambitions and go ahead with a more modest version of your plan.

Somewhere...somehow...there is a solution to your problem *if you only search for it.*

Who Gets to Keep the Muffin Tins?

During a business breakup, there are hundreds of potential problems to be overcome. Most of them deal with a division of the company's assets, which may include real estate, cash, equipment, materials, patents and copyrights, trademarks, inventory, the employees of the firm, and not to be overlooked, the customer lists and contracts.

When people go into business, it is always wise to delineate who "owns" what and whether that "owner" is transferring rights to the company as a condition of the business agreement.

Whenever possible, it is best to transfer such rights to the company, preferably in exchange for a financial consideration. That way, if a subsequent breakup occurs, things that are essential to the operation of the business, such as patents, will remain the property of the company and the departing "owner" must forfeit them upon leaving.

People Often Agree Not to Compete

Many people also sign noncompetitive agreements when a business is formed. In other words, they agree that a departing principal cannot start a competitive business or, in some cases, even go to work for a competing company for a specified period of time, usually anywhere from one to five years.

This protects the firm against someone who might walk away with valuable trade secrets or even make off with a good share of the company's customers. It also tends to make a person think twice before leaving the company.

Accept the Support of Your Family and Friends

Breaking up a business can be a very difficult and emotional time for anyone and everyone. It can make you edgy, bitter, sharp, and generally unpleasant. So you must be extra careful not to punish your family for what is going on at work.

One's family and friends are particularly important at times like this, and their support should be gratefully received and acknowledged.

Sometimes Bankruptcy Is the Only Answer

In extreme cases, bankruptcy isn't necessarily bad.

There are several types of bankruptcy, and you should know the differences.

Under *Chapter 7*, for example, the court assigns the company to a trustee who sells off the firm's assets and then the distributes the money to the firm's creditors.

Under *Chapter 11*, however, the law provides you with an opportunity to salvage your business by freezing the company's debts, including any pending lawsuits, while you formulate a plan to resolve your financial problems. As you are developing such a plan, your company remains in operation.

Generally, you will be given 120 days to devise your plan, although judges will often extend that deadline if they see that you are earnestly attempting to resolve your problems and believe that, with a little more time, you may be able to do that.

The Chapter 11 reorganization plan must detail how you foresee paying your creditors and how long you think that will take. The plan can involve the sale of certain assets, the reduction of overhead through various means, attempts to refinance, and so on, but it must be approved by both your creditors and the bankruptcy judge.

Sometimes creditors will be willing to accept 40 cents on the dollar (a 40 percent plan). Sometimes a plan assures the creditors of payment in full (a 100 percent plan). If the plan is approved, your company remains protected by law for as long as it takes you to implement it and pay off your creditors.

Whatever the terms of your plan, once they have been fulfilled to the satisfaction of the court, your firm no longer will be in bankruptcy and you will be free to resume normal operations—probably with a sharper, trimmer, more efficient approach than before.

Bankruptcy is the financial extreme, to be avoided if at all possible. But if bankruptcy seems inevitable, the provisions of Chapter 11 may provide you with some protection, additional time, and an opportunity to successfully salvage your business.

You should be aware of all the options that are available to you under the law.

Dividing the Assets Is Easier in a Corporation

Obviously, the breakup of a business is much less complicated when the firm has been incorporated. In such cases, all of the principals own a specific number of shares in the company, which represent a calculated percentage of the company's assets. Each person may then sell or retain those shares as he or she sees fit.

Compensating people for their holdings when they decide to leave the company can be accomplished in a number of ways:

1. Do nothing and let each person hold the shares, sell them, or do whatever they choose with them.
2. The remaining principal(s) can buy the shares.
3. Other potential investors—such as the company's employees—can buy the shares.
4. The company itself can buy the shares of the departing principal out of its retained earnings.

5. The company can be sold to another firm and the proceeds divided among the principals.

Or, the company can be sold in exchange for shares in the acquiring company, rather than cash, and those shares can be divided among the principals. If payment is made in the form of stock, naturally that stock represents cash and can be either held or sold as they wish.

In some cases, some of the principal(s) may remain in the business and take a position in the surviving company, while the others can take their cash and leave.

Who Will Determine the Value?

A partnership can be far more difficult to dissolve, even if the partnership agreement clearly specifies each principal's share of the business. For example:

How is the real estate to be evaluated and divided?

What value do you place on a second-hand typewriter or the company's good will?

Will certain assets have to be sold to pay off the departing principal? If so, which ones?

Is the departing principal willing to accept payment over a period of time, rather than all at once? Can you work out an acceptable payment schedule?

If the departing principal is willing to be bought out in installments, you have to pay interest on the unpaid balance? What rate is acceptable?

A Thought to Remember

He has achieved success who has lived well, laughed often and loved much.

—Bessie A. Stanley

It should be obvious that working out the details of a business breakup under amicable conditions will make the process much easier for everyone concerned. If bitterness prevails, however, it probably is best to let lawyers sort things out for you. That can be costly, but bitterness also has a price. A poor decision, hastily made, made in anger, or made out of stubbornness, misunderstanding, or lack of knowledge can be more costly than a lawyer's fees.

A business breakup, like a divorce, is not something that should be taken lightly.

Set your mind to one thought: Make every situation, every decision-making opportunity, every problem and solution a learning experience. Use each as a chance to strengthen your own knowledge and resolve and to forge from them a better, stronger, more profitable business for the future.

Chances are, the one who walks away from the business will lose more in the long run than the one who perseveres and fights on.

Chapter 9 Checkup

If It Happened to You...

Your business partner, an uncle, announces suddenly that he would like to leave the company.

1. What is the best argument that you could use to make him change his mind?

2. Are there any *other* reasons for him to change his mind?

3. If he is determined to go, and wants to take his assets with him, can you afford to buy him out?

4. Can you find *another* means of buying him out?

5. Can you find somebody else to handle his responsibilities within the company?

6. Have you considered how his departure might affect other people in the company? Your customers? Your suppliers? Other members of the family?

7. Have you asked him to stay on until you are able to work out a smooth transition?

10
The Fish
Out of Water

Business, as such, does not hold a bias of any kind—sexual, religious, educational, ethnic, age-related, or nationalistic.

One of the largest insurance companies in the South is owned by a black man.

A successful foundry operation in Ohio is run by a woman.

Some of the nation's largest dressmaking firms are headed by men.

One of the most prominent computer software companies was founded by a teenager.

One of the most prominent computer hardware companies was founded by an oriental.

A New Look at the Old Stereotypes

Prior to World War II, it was the popular conception that most Japanese products were cheap, tinny junk. Today, we buy billions of dollars worth of Japanese cars, cameras, television sets, computers, VCRs, heavy equipment, and dozens of other high-quality merchandise a year.

Today's Women Do It All

In Tucson, Arizona, Pam Furlong owns and operates three instant printing companies (AlphaGraphics).

In Florida, Sheila Guth is part owner of two stores that sell baseball cards and other sports-related memorabilia (Baseball Card Center).

In Cambridge, Massachusetts, Judi Wineland heads a company that creates, markets, and conducts exotic, adventurous trips to far-off countries (Overseas Adventure Travel).

In Oklahoma City, Oklahoma, Patty Hampton runs a Triple-A baseball team (the 89ers).

In San Rafael, California, Robin Bacci directs a profitable automobile dealership (Mercedes).

If these women surprise you by being successful in fields that you might have considered "men's work," then consider Ted Rice of Kansas City, Missouri, who sells sweet rolls (T.J. Cinnamons), or Richard Grassgreen of Montgomery, Alabama, who operates a chain of child care centers (Kinder-Care Learning Centers, Inc.).

Think about David Kimmel of New York City who, with his wife Martha, runs a firm that produces fresh baby food (Mommy Made), and Coleman Orr of Alphetta, Georgia, who has franchised a firm to clean house windows (Classic Care of America).

Women's work? Men's work? Not any more!

Once, a woman might have had trouble opening a charge account with her husband as a cosigner. Now, women as well as men are arranging six- and seven-figure bank loans in order to sustain their businesses.

The key to success today involves a good idea, lots of hard work and determination, and sound management. Forget the old stereotypes.

Government Regulations Designed to Aid Minorities

Once, a black or hispanic person might have had difficulty in starting and operating a business. Now the federal government has specific regulations that *mandate* the letting of contracts to minority-owned businesses.

Years ago, when an oriental opened a business in America, it probably was a restaurant or a laundry. Today, we find Orientals creating computer empires like that of Dr. An Wang (Wang Laboratories) or Bernie Tse (Wyse Technology).

We certainly are not blind to the fact that some biases do exist, even today, but they exist primarily in the minds of certain individuals and they are *not* inherent in business itself.

In today's society, everyone has an equal opportunity to get an idea, work hard, form a company, and seek their fortune.

You Can't Succeed If You Don't Try

Too often, I have found that people tend to let their own biases get in the way of success. "I'm a woman so they won't give me a chance," they'll say. Or, "I'm too young" ... "I'm too old" ... "I don't have enough education." These are not excuses for failure; they are excuses for not trying.

No businessperson, banker, or lawyer is saying, "We won't give you a chance." The individual is saying, "I'm afraid to try."

It is much easier for some people to say "I can't!" than to say "I will!"

Nobody can dispute the fact that you cannot succeed if you don't try. Nolan Bushnell, the founder of Atari, has created 14 companies, and six of them have failed.

You Needn't Wait to be Asked

I recently read about a well-known baseball player who took a walk on his day off and saw some children organizing a ball game in the neighborhood park. Stopping to watch, the athlete noticed a small boy standing to one side.

As the boys began to form teams, one of them asked the little fellow if he would like to play, but the boy simply shook his head.

Later, when a player had to leave the game, someone again asked the boy if he would like to play, and again he shook his head.

After awhile, the boy recognized the famous ballplayer who was standing near him and he asked for an autograph.

"Do you think I can grow up to be a famous baseball player like you?" the admiring youngster asked, clutching the treasured autograph in his hand.

"Yes," replied his new friend, "but first *you have to get in the game*."

Success is *never* guaranteed in business, but you don't even stand a chance if you don't get in the game.

Everything Seems Strange at First

It is worth remembering that everybody is a "fish out of water" when they are starting a new business. Success is not borne in the genes; it is something that you earn through hard work and experience, trial and error, win and lose.

You are most likely to succeed if you study your field well, learn as much as you can, plan as carefully as possible, and get the best advice you can. Least likely to succeed is someone who is totally unfamiliar with the field, acts on a whim, is underfinanced, and gambles on unreasoned hunches.

No one can hit a home run every time at bat, sink a hole-in-one on every golf shot, or take first prize whenever they play the lottery. You *will* fail at times, and you have no reason to expect otherwise. The thrill of success stems from having known the bitter taste of failure.

Vince Lombardi, who was famous for his success as the coach of the Green Bay Packers, once told his players: "You are going to get knocked down once in awhile. The secret to winning is to *get up and knock someone else down.*"

As successful as he was, Lombardi:

Never had a quarterback who could complete every pass.

Never had a running back who could score a touchdown on every carry.

Never had an undefeated season.

Lombardi knew the thrill of victory, but he also knew the agony of defeat.

Every Startup Requires Certain Preliminaries

So you're not Vince Lombardi... but you *do* have a desire to run your own business.

Is there anything you can do to offset that fish-out-of-water feeling?

Step 1: Study.

Go to the library and read everything you can find related to your prospective business. Don't overlook the magazines, particularly the trade magazines and the business journals.

The library can also tell you if your industry is served by a trade association or a professional society. If it is, get the address and write to them for information, suggestions, and a list of recommended literature to read. See if they sponsor seminars and training programs, or offer consulting services.

See if there are any franchisers in the field and, if so, see what they may have to offer.

Go to your local high school, trade school, business school, junior college, college, and university. See what courses they offer to increase your knowledge and sharpen your skills in the field that you are interested in.

Talk to successful business people in your field of interest. Ask lots of questions. Get detailed answers.

Step 2: Put your ideas on paper.

Describe exactly what you propose to do and *how* you plan to do it. Go into as much detail as possible.

As you are doing this, questions are bound to arise. Go back to step 1 and do more research until all of your questions are answered.

The hardest part will be explaining how you plan to achieve your goal.

How will you finance it?

Will you need an office, store, factory, or warehouse? If so, how large a one?

How many employees will you need?

Will you need equipment? How much? What kind?

Who will your suppliers be. Your customers? Your competition? Describe them all.

Step 3: Prepare a business plan.

Go back to step 2 and, using that as your guide, flesh out your plan for starting a business. Put a timetable and a cost on everything that needs to be done.

What must you do first? Second?

What is the earliest you can possibly get started on implementing your plan?

What is the earliest you can possibly have your business in operation?

What is the earliest that you can reasonably expect the business to show a profit?

If you need an office, store, or factory, do you have a site in mind? Is it available? What will it cost?

If you need equipment, what kind? Where can you get it? What will it cost? How long will it take to get delivery and have it installed?

If you know who your suppliers will be, do you know their prices? Their delivery schedules? (If you do not know who your suppliers will be, you had better find out, and line up some alternates as well, just in case.)

If you know who your customers will be, how do you plan to reach them? Will you advertise? How much? Where?

Why should your customers patronize you, rather than one of your competitors?

How much money will you have to spend before you can generate your first income? Where will you get that money? Have you planned to set aside a little more, just in case of some unexpected snag?

How long will it be before you can realistically expect to generate a sufficient amount of cash flow? Do you have enough funds to see you through until that time?

Are you sure that the anticipated cash flow will be enough to cover all your expenses...plus a profit?

Step 4: Test-fly your idea.

Show some people your plan and ask for their opinions. Your family is a good place to start, even if they are not very familiar with the industry. If they ask a question that you can't answer, get the answer and work it into your plan.

Be sure your family is objective and gives you a full and honest appraisal of your plan, not simply something that they think you want to hear. Assure them that negative comments will not offend you and that, in fact, you want them to play devil's advocate. Assure them that you want their true feelings and opinions on the matter.

After you have smoothed out your plan so that it leaves none of your questions unanswered, and it satisfies the most skeptical member of your family, try it out on other people that you trust and respect. Let a lawyer look at it, an accountant, your banker, or someone who is familiar with the field in question. If it passes their scrutiny, you should have a reasonably complete, accurate, and well-detailed plan.

Step 5: Get going.

Start, but start cautiously. Take things one step at a time, and be patient. Do not try to speed things up by taking shortcuts or by jumping ahead of your preestablished timetable.

If you encounter something that is outside the parameters established in your plan, stop and make the necessary adjustments *throughout the plan.*

If, for example, you had expected to rent a storefront for $15.00 a square foot and the owner has raised the rate to $17.50 a square foot, be sure to recheck your figures to see if you can afford the added cost. If not, you may have to locate another, less expensive site.

Do not "rob Peter to pay Paul." Your plan should be based on a carefully selected set of circumstances—things that you can measure and control, at least to some extent. If you attempt to compensate for an increase in rent by reducing the amount of equipment you will purchase, for example, your entire plan may begin to disintegrate like a house of cards, one element collapsing beneath the weight of another.

Implement your business plan like you would if you had been planning a motor trip. In business, the "fuel" that propels you is the amount of money that you have to invest. If you run out of it, you may find yourself literally stranded by the side of the road. Try to reach each milepost on time and on budget, and try to avoid any detours.

The New Kid on the Block

We do not plan to ignore the fact that many people who are new to business do not start from scratch.

Many of those who join an existing family business for the first time also tend to feel like a fish out of water—at least for a time. Spouse of the owner, child of the owner, whatever the relationship, they often feel like they are being put under a microscope when they take a place in the company.

If that is happening to you, what can you do to ease the discomfort and win your co-workers' acceptance?

My first recommendation is that you learn as much about the business as you can before you start to work. Go to the sources listed under step 1 for first-time entrepreneurs earlier in this chapter. Do all of the things that are listed there, and also ask the person who will be your supervisor to give you a thorough briefing.

Once on the job, introduce yourself to the other employees or as many of them as practical. Find out what *they* do and tell them what *you* will be doing. Admit that you are new and inexperienced, and ask for their help. Everyone's ego gets a boost when asked for help.

Work as hard as you can to establish your worth in the company. Show that you can do your job and do it well.

Ask a Classmate, Not the Teacher

If you run into a problem, go to a co-worker for help, rather than the boss. Show the other employees that you are independent, that you aren't going to run to a relative when you have problems, and that you welcome and appreciate the help of your peers.

You may not be fully accepted by the other employees until you do run into a spot of trouble. The manner in which you handle yourself at that time will determine the standard by which the other employees will measure you in the future. Handle the situation well and you will be "in"; handle it poorly and you may have a rough time winning the other workers' acceptance.

Don't Try to Be a 90-Day Wonder

Assume additional responsibilities gradually. Do not bite off more than you can chew. Show your co-workers that you are deserving of each advancement and you will win their support. People who move from the mail room to a vice presidency in less than two weeks will always be suspect among the other workers.

Remember that your co-workers have families too. They want their children to get ahead and they are pulling for you to succeed as well. But they want to see you move upward on your merit, not on your family ties; otherwise they will feel that you have sidestepped the system and betrayed their set of values.

Although you may have high ambitions of your own, do not take advantage of family relationships to "climb the ladder" over those who have invested more time and energy in the company than you have and who may be far more deserving of promotion than you are. Be patient; wait your turn.

Prove that you have what it takes to be a leader. Remember that you will need the support of your co-workers in the future, no matter how far in the company you may go.

Help the Company, Help Yourself

A good rule of thumb is to always act in the best interest of the company. You can't be faulted for that; if the company prospers, everyone will prosper.

When young, immature, inexperienced, and/or incapable people move to the top of any company, it has been my observation that nobody benefits.

The Time to Move Ahead

At some point, your grandparent, parent, aunt, or uncle—whoever is at the head of the company—may want to move you upward before you are ready. Resist that temptation. If you accept it and perform poorly, you will disappoint both them and yourself; but if you reject the offer on the grounds that you are not yet ready for the responsibility, you will earn their respect, your own, and that of your co-workers.

If you think about it, you will realize that you will not be fulfilled, and you will not be happy, in any position where you cannot perform adequately. Regardless of the allure of a nice title, some extra money, or the family encouragement, you must be able to convince yourself that you are doing a good job or you will never be satisfied.

In the long run, it is not the title or the salary that matters; it is how well you can handle the job. If you advance beyond your capabilities, there is a good chance that you will not hold the title or receive the salary for very long.

Your relatives want you to succeed. You want to succeed. And in their hearts, the other employees want you to succeed. Acknowledge their support and win their respect by advancing at your own rate of speed.

From individual to individual, the rate of ascent varies. Some people learn more quickly than others. Some are more competent than others. The fault is not with the slow learner or the less competent person, but with their failure to recognize their limitations and conduct themselves accordingly.

Learn to judge your own capabilities. You may be able to fool other people for a time, but it will be hard for you to fool yourself. Remember that you share the family responsibility to protect the business, the employees, and the customers to the best of your ability. If, by trying to do too much too soon, you damage the business, then you may also damage your relatives, the other employees, and the customers upon whom your future depends.

Nepotism: Neither Villainy Nor Virtue

I have never been either an opponent or a proponent of nepotism. I have seen it succeed, and I have seen it fail.

Nepotism has been most successful, by my observation, when it has been practiced judiciously, monitored carefully, and implemented slowly. It has failed most often when the older generation has thrown caution to the winds, ignored the need for adequate training and experience, delegated too much too soon, and failed to monitor the younger generation in a manner that is likely to assure success.

Too frequently, the boss who is overly strict with non family members will be overly lenient with members of the family. It is a mistake to have a dual set of standards—one for "us" and another for "them."

You *Are* Being Watched

Entering a family business for the first time, you are indeed under a microscope. Everyone above you, below you, and around you will be watching to see how well you conduct yourself.

They will assume that they can do whatever you do. Arrive late for work and they will feel that they can arrive late also. Leave early and they will feel that they can leave early too. Do a haphazard job and they will do a haphazard job.

Set a good example and they will follow it.

Ability and Dedication Do Count

Ability and dedication are the benchmarks against which you will be measured, whether you are starting a new business or entering an existing one.

If you have those qualities, your associates will recognize it and respect it. If you are lacking in either one, they will respond accordingly. Both attitudes work hand in glove. If you have ability but lack dedication, or have dedication but are lacking in ability, you will not be the kind of contributor that your associates can admire and follow.

You should work to develop and demonstrate both of these capabilities.

You *Can* Measure Your Own Dedication

Taking stock of a person's dedication isn't as simple as taking one's temperature.

People put on many disguises in life—even before themselves. Certainly, we try to hide ourselves from other people. It is a defense mechanism, I suppose, designed to help us cover up the things that we believe are flaws in our makeup.

Few of us truly know ourselves—what makes us do what we do, think what we think, act the way we act. Even if we attempted to be perfectly frank with ourselves, it probably wouldn't work.

How then do you find out whether you are truly dedicated to your work and your responsibilities, or simply going through the motions?

1. *Think of yourself as one of your own employees.*

If you were to rate your performance—as one employee among all the others—would you rate it high, low, or average? If it isn't at least average, perhaps you're not really happy with your work. You probably lack enthusiasm, and that's a good indication that you lack dedication as well.

2. *Look at the things for which you are personally responsible.*

Is your work getting done? Is it on time? Is it being done well?

If your work is stacking up, if deadlines are being missed, if people are complaining because your work is sloppy or haphazard, then you're probably either overworked or just goofing off.

If you're overworked, perhaps you need to hire someone to share your workload. Better to delegate the work to someone else than to develop a reputation for poor performance.

If you're goofing off, take stock of your dedication.

Chapter 10 Checkup

Getting Yourself Ready

1. Name a trade journal that serves your industry.

   _____

2. Name a trade association or professional society that serves your industry.

   _____

3. Name a company that sells franchises in your field.

   _____

4. List three college-level courses that could help you in your business.

   _____

   _____

   _____

11
Family and "Outsiders" *Can* Mix

Family businesses sometimes tend to become terribly inbred. Exercising dubious judgment, many entrepreneurs tend to employ *any* member of the family, regardless of his or her interest, ability, or moral standards, and to shun *all* "outsiders." They give a number of reasons:

- You can trust members of the family.
- It keeps the money in the family.
- Aunt Norma would never forgive me if I don't give Jeffrey a job.

Excuses, Not Reasons

None of these arguments will hold water, of course.

The first excuse presumes that everyone outside the family is dishonest and unreliable, which is ridiculous. It also presupposes that every member of the family is honest and dependable, which is equally unreasonable.

The second argument has some merit in a small company. But if a business is to grow and prosper, it will require an increasing number of employees. So sooner or later it will become necessary to hire people from outside the family.

Furthermore, this argument suggests that a member of the family will work harder and more efficiently than an outsider will, and that may not be the case at all. Clearly, an industrious outsider may generate more money for the family than a poorly motivated relative.

Don't Look For Slave Labor

It is often easy for me to conclude that some entrepreneurs stick with family employees because they can pay the relative less than they would have to pay someone else.

If that were true—and if the relatives were willing to accept such slave labor treatment—I suppose it would be OK, especially during the startup period when dollars are often scarce.

On the other hand, I tend to subscribe to the theory that you get what you pay for, and paying a substandard wage to any employee does not provide much of an incentive, whether that employee is a relative or not.

Watch Out for Aunt Norma!

Dealing with Aunt Norma and her son Jeffrey is a personal issue, and I talked about various aspects of nepotism in the previous chapter.

If Aunt Norma presents you with "an offer you can't refuse," then I suppose you will have to cope with the issue. On the other hand, I'm sometimes inclined to think that certain entrepreneurs stay with employees from within the family simply because *it's easier than advertising for, screening, and training other help.* If so, then they're certainly shirking their responsibility toward the business, and that probably will come back to haunt them later.

Don't Blame Me!

It's even possible that entrepreneurs who are looking for the easy way out may find it convenient to use their relatives as an alibi for poor performance. If an outsider is hired and does not work out well, the entrepreneur must shoulder the blame; after all, the boss hired the outsider instead of hiring good ol' Jeffrey. But if the entrepreneur does hire Jeffrey, and Jeffrey does not work out well, then Jeffrey and Aunt Norma must take the blame.

Us Against Them

In some situations, it will be harder to prove yourself than in others.

Remember that business itself knows no bias, but the ones with whom you will be working may harbor some individual biases of their own, such as an us-against-them attitude toward management. Such sentiments are sometimes hard to identify and even harder to overcome, but they will eventually disappear as you demonstrate your ability and your dedication to the job.

Education, experience, and family background are the strongest influences in creating, as well as eliminating, biases. It will be more difficult for a woman to overcome the biases of her co-workers on the factory floor, for example, than it will be in the business office.

Realizing that most people have some bias of one form or another, you should be careful not to let your biases color your judgment, either.

Biases Can Serve As an Alibi

A reasonably subdued and "harmless" bias can easily emerge as an excuse for poor performance.

Young people, for example, may find it a convenient alibi to say, "They won't give me a chance because I'm too young." In reality, those young people may simply be lacking the ability, the experience, or the commitment to have earned the opportunity that they are seeking.

Their superiors had no bias against youth; after all, they hired the young people in the first place. The young people were simply using their own type of bias as an excuse for their own shortcomings.

If You're Prepared, You'll Need No Excuse

I remember an incident related to me by a business associate. It had to do with a young Jewish fellow who worked for him in the advertising and public relations department of a large firm in the West. It was a particularly busy period, and the department was understaffed. So my friend asked his subordinate to handle an especially pressing assignment, even though the man was new and relatively inexperienced.

On the day the program was to be presented for management approval, my friend was still swamped with work. So he said, "Ted, I know you've never made a presentation to management, but I'm buried in work and can't take the time to present your program. Besides, you created the program, so you are the best one to present it."

Ted left my friend's office with a large smile on his face and the glow in his eyes that comes from feeling that your superior has just paid you a high compliment.

About an hour later, when he returned, Ted's face told a different story.

"How did it go?" my friend asked.

"Terrible," replied the subordinate. "They tore the program apart!"

"Why?" my friend inquired.

"I don't know," Ted replied. "I guess they just didn't like me." He paused for a moment and then added: "I'm Jewish, you know."

"Ted," responded my friend, "close the door and sit down. I think we need to talk."

Ted closed the door and slumped into a chair.

"Tell me honestly, Ted," my friend began. "How do *you* feel about your program? Do you think it's the best you can do? If so, we'll go back in there right now and put up a fight with those guys."

Ted thought for a few minutes and then said, "Well, if I'd had another week to work on it and maybe another $5,000 in the budget, I think I might have done better."

"OK," my friend responded. "We can spare the additional $5,000, and I'll give you another week. Fix up your program the way you think it ought to be and then come back to me."

When Ted returned a week later, my friend made a point of being even busier than before.

"Ted, I'd planned to present your program to management this morning," he said, "but I simply can't get away right now. You present it ... and don't worry about it. Just give it your best shot."

When Ted left the office this time, he looked like a man who had been sentenced to jail. But when he returned an hour later, he wore a smile from ear to ear.

"How did it go?" my friend inquired.

"Great!" Ted beamed. "They think the program is terrific!"

My friend rose, walked around his desk, and closed the office door.

"Sit down a second, Ted," he said.

Ted took a chair.

"I lied to you this morning, Ted," my friend confessed. "I could have made that presentation with you, but I wanted you to do it yourself."

A look of bewilderment crossed Ted's face. My friend continued.

"Last week, you told me that management shot down your program because they didn't like you, possibly because of you're a member of a minority. Then you admitted that you'd gone into the meeting with a program that, in your own opinion, was something less than your best work. You improved on the program during this past week, and management has approved it."

My friend paused while Ted absorbed what was being said. Then he went on, "The point I'm trying to make is this: When you took an inferior program to management, they rejected it. You knew it had faults and they knew it had faults. Their decision had nothing to do with you as a person, and it certainly had nothing to do with your religion.

"When you offered them a good program today, you knew it was good and they knew it was good. That's why they approved it—not because they liked you, and not because of the church you go to. They approved it because *you gave them a good program!*"

They say that every story should have a happy ending, and this story is no exception.

Ted has maintained contact with my friend during the 25 years since this incident occurred.

For several years, they worked together as student and mentor, and Ted turned out some outstanding work. Since then, my friend has retired and Ted has gone on to become a highly respected executive with another West Coast firm.

Ted no longer looks for excuses and alibis; he now relies on his ability and dedication to his work.

Outsiders Can Create a Balance

When a company is composed solely of employees from within the family, it tends to transfer the family pecking order into the workplace. The dominant member around the house becomes the dominant individual on the job. The family "baby" continues to remain the baby. Household responsibilities become on-the-job responsibilities without consideration that the individuals involved may be capable of making far greater contributions.

Outsiders in the company tend to have a leavening effect. They give you an impartial yardstick against which to measure the performance of your relatives. Since they do not know or care about your family dynamics, they respond to each member of the family according to his or her individual merit, never mind who is dominant at home, who is oldest or youngest, who does this or who does that around the household.

Enhance the Spirit of Competition

Most significantly, perhaps, outsiders within the company create a competitive atmosphere; and competition is good for the growth of the business. Knowing that they are outsiders, they know that they must compete against relatives for salary, for promotion, for recognition. At the same time, the relatives become more competitive too because they do not want to be outshone by an outsiders.

You can—and should—capitalize on that spirit of competition through sales contests, Employee-of-the-Month awards, and similar techniques.

Outsiders who are not employees make a contribution to your success every day. Such helpful contributors include your banker, lawyer and accountant, consultants, your customers and suppliers. If they can be useful, why shouldn't outsiders within the company be useful?

Teamwork Should Be the Goal

Family members and outsiders do not have to be adversaries, nor should they be. Everyone in the company should consider themselves—and their co-workers—as members of a team, and virtually everyone agrees that people must work together if they're to make a winning team.

Family members in particular should welcome the contributions of outsiders. After all, the outsider is generally working for wages and not a piece of the action as most family members do.

To encourage good performance, it is effective to reward an employee with courtesy and cooperation as well as with money. It's also less expensive.

Management should always stress teamwork and take steps to replace anyone who refuses to act accordingly.

Promote According to Merit

The same problems that follow the policy of employing only relatives can often be found in a company that adheres too stringently to a promote-from-within policy. In both situations, the inclination to shut out "outsiders" prevents the company from participating in a flow of new ideas and a refreshing infusion of new blood.

Preparing the Next Generation

In any business environment, it is necessary to have leaders and to have followers.

Many entrepreneurs eventually will turn over the reins of their companies to their children, who should have had the experience of being good followers before they assume the responsibility of leadership. These children are the heirs of leadership, and they are fortunate to have the opportunity to learn the business and the elements of management from a parent mentor.

But this intrafamily progression also contains an element of weakness: Learning "at the knee" of one's parents, a child may absorb not only the parent's best capabilities, but the worst as well. The tendency is to do things the way they always have been done—not to make waves. There is an inclination to maintain the status quo and to take a skeptic's view of new methods, new concepts, or new technology. As a result, the second generation may find that it is taking charge of an already declining business and is inheriting the responsibility for turning it around or leading it the rest of the way downhill.

_____ **FAMILY SUCCESS SCENARIO 60** _____

FROST, INC.
Grand Rapids, Michigan

Frost, Inc. is a 74-year-old company that had been in the family for four generations before Chad Frost entered the firm. His father Ruben was the company's president at that time.

Chad had worked in the business for two years while going to school, but after he graduated from college he had opted to go into the aerospace industry with Textron. He stayed with Textron for three years.

In 1970, at the request of his father, Chad joined the family business. The firm has acquired a company in Cleveland, and Chad's father needed someone who could manage it. Chad accepted the challenge, and by 1972 the subsidiary was in good enough shape to be integrated into the company's main operations.

Ruben Frost then asked his son to become general manager of the parent company. Although the firm was losing money, Chad reluctantly accepted. He quickly discovered that he had inherited a mess. The plant was filthy and scrap was laying around in piles. The machinery was antiquated and the management was inept. Chad's father and the other relatives were avoiding change and even avoided making decisions.

Over the next year, Chad improved the plant's efficiency, increased sales enough to get the company back into the black, and — over many objections — hired a few professional managers from outside the family.

Ruben was impressed by his son's performance, but the other relatives, many of whom faced the prospect of losing their jobs, rebelled.

Ruben and Chad established a line of credit at the bank and bought out the other family members. By 1977, they had restructured Frost's ownership. Some preferred stock was set aside for Chad's brother and sisters; Ruben and Chad kept the rest. Ruben was the majority shareholder, but Chad, now elevated to the office of president, was given an option to buy out his father at a later date.

Progress came slowly.

Ruben stepped aside in 1981.

Chad attempted to diversify the company's product line, only to discover that the engineers couldn't design new products, the shop couldn't produce them, and the sales force couldn't sell them.

Chad took drastic action. After appointing an acting chief executive officer to look after the company, Chad spent two years studying automated plants in the United States and Japan. Consultants told him it would cost between $12 million and $15 million to automate his plant, but Chad persisted.

Resuming his role as company president in 1983, Chad began to install automated equipment, completing the job at a cost of just $5 million.

Surveying the company's management structure, he abolished 11 formal and six informal layers of management and replaced it with a simple four-tier arrangement.

Time clocks were removed.

A new cafeteria was built, along with a wellness center.

Almost one-third of the company's staff was given professional outplacement counseling. All of the remaining employees were given an opportunity to become shareholders, were put on a productivity-based bonus plan, and were given profit-sharing benefits.

An employee training program was created.

With the new automated equipment, Frost's performance improved. Where it took 12 hours to reset the old machines, it took only a few minutes to convert the new ones. Where quality control previously rejected one out of four pieces, it now rejected only one out of 200. Where sales per employee had run $80,000 per year, it jumped to $150,000 a year.

Between 1983 and 1986, Frost's sales increased 30 percent and gross margins doubled.

Chad Frost was recognized as Michigan's 1985 Innovation Advocate of the Year by the Small Business Administration.

Learn Outside the Family Business

Many parents have realized that their children should not continue to run things in the same old way in view of rapidly changing modern business conditions. In some cases, they have rejected the idea of taking their children into the family business too soon, and they have insisted that their children work in other companies first. In that way, the younger generation is exposed to other management styles, other operating philosophies, and a variety of other business situations while their minds are still open and *before* they enter the family business.

It's a Calculated Risk

There is a danger in this approach: If the children enter another company, like it, and do well there, they may not want to leave that company in order to enter the family business. You will have lost your heir successors, but you will have the satisfaction of knowing that your children are happy and doing well.

Sometimes, either a customer or a supplier will be happy to win your favor by giving your offspring a job. This can provide valuable training for the time when the child eventually joins the family business. It's an excellent way of gaining experience, and it costs nothing. On the contrary, it can help you to strengthen your ties with the customer or supplier involved, assuming, of course, that your children do well while in the other company.

Learn Inside the Family Business

An in-house means of achieving the same purpose is to make good use of outsider talent. If you hire skilled, capable people for important middle- and upper-management positions, you can then apprentice your children to them.

Bear in mind, however, that this approach will be only as effective as you allow it to be.

You must hire good people, you must give them the opportunity to run their departments as they see fit, and you must allow them to interface with your children without interference.

The in-house approach is not likely to produce the desired results if you:

- Hire people who are simply a mirror of your own management style and philosophy.

- Hamstring your executives with rules and regulations that restrict their creativity.

- Reject attempts to introduce improvements or explore new technologies.

- Fail to allow your subordinates the chance to deal freely, openly, and without fear of reprisal while they are working with your children.

Corporate America's Loss Can Be Your Gain

It is increasingly rare for large corporations to hire older people. Indeed the current trend is toward increased automation, trimmer overhead, fewer layers of management, and numerous corporate mergers, which is putting many older executives out of work.

This can be a great benefit to the family-owned business.

Let us assume that you own a business and your heir apparent needs a good five years of experience and training in marketing before taking on a major management position in the company. At the same time, you hear of a well-functioning firm in your field that has just been acquired by a conglomerate that plans to release many of its seasoned executives.

You contact their top marketing executive with a proposal: Join your company on a five-year contract, help to train your heir in marketing during those five years, and then step aside, making room for the heir, who should now be ready to assume the responsibility.

Such an offer can be very appealing to someone in the 50- to 65-year-old age bracket, for a number of reasons:

It's flattering to have been sought out and offered a responsible position.

The new employee realizes that there are few good job opportunities for people of his age.

He or she can move into the new position without going through the sometimes lengthy, often demeaning process of preparing a resume, answering ads, and submitting to job interviews.

It is ego-building to be entrusted with the responsibility of training an heir successor.

It means five years of guaranteed employment, as well as time to prepare for eventual retirement.

The offer can be sweetened in a number of ways. For example, you can suggest a salary plus a performance-based bonus, or you can contribute to an annuity that will provide the executive with an income after retirement.

If you are not fortunate enough to have such a tailor-made candidate laid at your doorstep, you can seek one out. Watch the Job Wanted ads in *The Wall Street Journal*, major trade publications, and similar media, for example. If you don't find an appealing prospect, place your own ad in one or more of those same publications. Eventually, you will find the right person for the job.

This arrangement creates a marvelous win-win situation in which everybody benefits.

You get the services of a well qualified marketing expert.

Your heir successor gets a top-notch mentor.

Your "temporary" employee gets a job, some financial security, and a boost to the ego.

Coincidentally, you avoid some potentially touchy personnel problems. Your new employee does not feel threatened by your heir because it is known from the outset that your heir will be the successor in five years, and because there is a contract that assures the new employee of five years' security. Your heir successor doesn't feel bypassed, overlooked, or threatened either, because it is understood that he (or she) will take over in five years.

As a result, the working relationship between the two individuals — teacher and student — should be as smooth as silk.

This is an excellent example of the ways in which outsiders can make major contributions to a family-owned business.

Hire an Outsider or Promote from Within?

There are many philosophical debates about which is better: to promote from within or to hire a capable outsider. I have never understood why this should be an either/or situation or why it has to be painted only in black or white. The answer, to me, is to keep an open mind to both options.

If you have hired good people, trained them well, and positioned them properly, there should be a well-qualified individual ready to fill any vacancy that occurs. So it should be easy — and would make good sense — to promote them when the opportunities exist.

On the other hand, only a very large company can afford to be three-deep in every position, and it does take time to train a person adequately. So if you are unfortunate enough to lose several people from the same department over a short period, you may have no alternative but to fill a position by hiring someone from the outside.

Diversified Company, Diversified Work Force

Other occasions that call for hiring an outsider may occur when your company diversifies or acquires a subsidiary. In such cases, there simply may not be any qualified people within the company to fill the new and unfamiliar positions that have been created. The surest, easiest, and quickest way to develop the needed staff is to hire outsiders.

Make Policies That Apply to Everyone

Two ever present areas of conflict in a family business involve the questions of salaries and promotions. Nothing is more likely to create dissent than paying one individual more than another when both are doing comparable work, or having to choose between two individuals when it is time to announce a promotion.

The best way to avoid such conflict is to formulate a clear-cut policy regarding salaries and promotions *and then stick to it*, whether the individuals involved are members of the family or not.

Be aware that there are other ways to reward an employee than with money or a promotion. You can use them to maintain a happy balance, when necessary. These include, but are not restricted to:

Carefully selected time off

An award, such as a certificate or plaque

A business trip to some desirable location

A transfer of workload

More help on the job

A lateral "promotion" to another job or location

More vacation time

The use of a company car

A larger or more attractive office or work situation

New office furniture or furnishings

A noncompensated increase in responsibility

All of these and many other things of a like nature may be used to reward exceptional performance without upsetting the salary scale, the promotion policy, or the overall balance of your organization. If they are to serve their purpose, however, rewards of this type must be used with discretion and must be treated seriously.

Avoid Becoming a Party to a Dispute

Try to avoid direct participation in a dispute between employees, particularly when one of them is a relative. Delegate that sort of thing to someone else, and let it be known that the decision of the individual you have chosen will be final. If the person you have named is not a member of the family, their decision stands a greater likelihood of being impartial or at least of giving the impression of impartiality.

Do not make the mistake of trying to cluster your employees. That is, do not put all your relatives in one department and all the outsiders in another, all the old-timers in one group and all of the young Turks in another, all the women here and all the men there.

A good diversity will produce a good dynamic—the older employees, for example, will teach experience, patience, and conservatism to the younger ones; the younger ones will stimulate their older associates with their enthusiasm, vigor, and fresh ideas.

Chapter 11 Checkup

From Generation to Generation

1. List five of your parents' business policies that you would prefer to change.

_____

_____

_____

2. Tell *how* you would change each of those policies.

_____

_____

_____

3. Tell *why* you would change each policy as you have suggested.

_____

_____

_____

12
Letting Go

Over the years, your business has grown. Your children have grown. You are beginning to think about when and how to "let go," turn things over to someone else, retire.

You have learned that the rigors of running a business don't disappear as you get older and wiser or as the company gets larger and more complex. The problems tend only to grow larger and more complex.

As the Company Has Grown, You Have Grown

Perhaps you have been too busy to notice how your style of management has changed over the years. When you were starting up, you were a jack of all trades—a one-man band. Later, you recognized the need to delegate some of the work, so you began to form a management team and to share the load.

A Thought to Remember

In the wide arena of the world, failure and success are not accidents as we so frequently suppose, but the strictest justice. If you do your fair day's work, you are certain to get your fair day's wage—in praise or pudding, whichever happens to suit your taste.

Alexander Smith

Startups Get the Adrenalin Going

To many entrepreneurs, the startup phase is the most fun. It's creative. It's dynamic. It's daring. It's the most "responsive"—the time when even minor successes show up most quickly and most dramatically.

Some never get beyond that startup stage. Such people need that kind of excitement, and never learn to delegate or to work with a team. As a result, they generally fail to attain their true growth potential.

Don't Hang Around Too Long

Under the best of circumstances, persons will decide for themselves when it is time to step aside. They will give the matter a great deal of thought, work out a comfortable timetable, and even plan what they will do after they leave the company.

Unfortunately, not all entrepreneurs are that wise or farsighted. Some stay on far longer than they should, fail to provide for an effective transition to a new management, and fail to plan as carefully for the *end* of their business career as they did for the *beginning* of it.

As a result, they frequently fail to get as much for their company as it is worth, and even more frequently leave the business in an organizational shambles.

You'll See the Warning Signs, If You're Looking

It isn't easy to walk away from a company that you created, nurtured through good times and bad, and watched as it grew throughout the years. The business becomes a way of life and assumes a personality of its own.

How can you tell if you have stayed on too long? Watch for one or more of these warning signs:

- Are you getting bored? Paying less attention to business than you used to?
- Are your associates bypassing you and making critical business decisions on their own?
- Is your product or service becoming obsolete?
- Are your competitors growing while you seem to be standing still?
- Are you beginning to feel that you no longer understand the business because of new technology or changing market conditions?

- Are larger companies buying up your competitors, leaving you as one of the few remaining independents?
- Is your plant becoming antiquated? Your staff too old?

Any of these might be a signal that you have stayed on too long and that it is time to consider stepping aside.

You Have Lots of Options

Fortunately, one's separation from a business does not have to be total and immediate. Retirement is not like giving up cigarettes; people do not have to go cold turkey unless they want to. They are many alternates from which to choose.

Stepping Down But Not Out

When the company has grown enough to be attractive to some of the larger corporations, you may have to choose between going it alone or becoming part of a bigger operation, as Kingsley Morse did.

In the 1960s, Morse founded his one-route air taxi service, Command Airways, in Poughkeepsie, New York. The carrier grew into a substantial regional airline over the next quarter century. In 1985, the company carried over 250,000 passengers and took in $15.7 million in revenues.

But the trend in aviation these days is for the large airlines to absorb the smaller competitors. And although Morse resisted for awhile, he was finally convinced that "if you can't lick 'em, join 'em."

In May 1986, Morse signed a marketing agreement with American Air Lines and became one of that carrier's American Eagle affiliates.

_____ **FAMILY SUCCESS SCENARIO 61** _____

LONGMAN GROUP USA
Chicago, Illinois

About the time Morse was founding Command Airways, Robert Kyle was borrowing $5,000 to form a publishing company in Chicago.

Kyle had written a real estate textbook, which he eventually parlayed into a nationally acclaimed training and publishing firm with 45 employees and $5 million a year in sales.

Suitors came calling—Prentice-Hall, CBS, McGraw-Hill.

Kyle rejected all offers until he was approached by England's Longman Group Ltd., a subsidiary of the $1.6 billion Pearson Plc.

Longman offered Kyle $5 million for his company and the opportunity to become head of Longman Group USA in Chicago.

Since then, Kyle has added over 20 other companies to the group, which employs over 550 people in 17 offices, and he has made his operation Longman's fastest growing division, producing some $70 million a year in sales.

Freedom and Fun, but with a Financial Interest

It is possible to achieve several things simultaneously: freedom from the pressures of managing the company, some immediate financial return, and a stake in the future growth of the firm as well.

_____ **FAMILY SUCCESS SCENARIO 62** _____

THOUSAND TRAILS, INC. (SOUTHMARK CORP.)
Dallas, Texas

Another entrepreneur of the 1960s, Milton Kuolt II enjoyed being outdoors in his travel trailer, but he found most campgrounds overcrowded, poorly maintained, and frequently unsafe.

Kuolt founded Thousand Trails, Inc., a company that offered trailer pads in scenic locations with a clubhouse, a pool, and other comforts.

He began by clearing the first sites with the help of his children and built Thousand Trails into the country's largest chain of membership campgrounds:

19 preserves in five states and British Columbia in 1981

27,600 members

900 employees

$40 million a year in sales

$3.3 million a year in profits

But by the early 1980s, Kuolt felt that he was losing control. After a year of agonizing over his decision, he engaged someone else to run the company, sold most of his stock, and left the company.

Three entrepreneurs. Three sets of circumstances. Three different solutions.

Bad Decisions Produce
Bad Results

Not all situations work out favorably.

Sam, Ben, and Abe Itkin founded an office furniture business in New York City in 1934. Through hard work and determination, the business grew. Abe handled the financial side of the operation while Sam and Ben took charge of sales. During the 1950s, the company produced $3 million a year in sales. By 1964, sales had climbed to $5 million.

Meanwhile, Ben's son Lewis entered the company, to be followed by Abe's son Leonard and Sam's two sons, Larry and David. As sales hit $8 million in 1974, the boys took an increasingly active role in the management of the company.

When Abe and Ben Itkin retired, Sam bought them out and announced that it was his intention to leave the company to the four boys in equal shares.

Sam's sons resented that agreement and left the company. So when Sam retired a year and a half later, he left the business in the hands of his two nephews.

Almost immediately, things began to change:

The refinishing business was eliminated.

The reupholstering business was dropped.

Key accounts were lost.

Long-time employees were fired.

The product line deteriorated in quality.

Finally, they changed the name of the company.

In April 1986, the Itkin company was liquidated.

Sometimes There's a Family Feud

The Horvitz family fared no better. Samuel Horvitz, who had started his career selling newspapers on a street corner at the age of eight, died in 1956, leaving a $700 million estate that included five newspapers, nine cable television companies, a construction company, and $70 million worth of Florida real estate.

Horvitz also left three sons: Harry, who took over the management of the media properties; Leonard, who assumed control of the construction company; and William, who became head of the real estate interests.

Some 20 years later, Hattie Horvitz, the boys' mother, died.

Within months, Leonard and William worked out a plan to take the profits from Harry's newspapers and to use them for their own companies.

Harry sued. The in-fighting, lawsuits, and bitterness raged on for nearly ten years. Eventually, all of the Horvitz assets were sold so that the proceeds could be divided among the sons three ways.

Watch Out for the Unexpected

Serious problems frequently occur when the unexpected happens, in spite of everyone's good intentions.

In 1970, for example, Joyce Signer was a contented housewife, intent on raising her son and two daughters. Signer's husband was in the process of buying a General Motors dealership in Corvallis, Oregon.

Then her husband died of a heart attack.

When it was learned that the husband's will called for the business to be sold and the proceeds placed in a trust, Signer went to court to have the will set aside. It was, and she subsequently has become owner and operator of the successful Signer Motors, Inc.

Essie Askew could empathize with Joyce Signer.

─────────────── **FAMILY SUCCESS SCENARIO 63** ───────────────

ASKEW DISTRIBUTING CO.
Chicago, Illinois

In 1980, Askew's husband James died unexpectedly, leaving her to run the family business. Askew Distributing Co. was a fledgling beer distributorship that was losing about $20,000 a year.

There were debts, which Essie paid off with funds from her husband's insurance.

She trimmed the company's overhead in order to improve its cash flow.

She slashed her own income, and the company controller agreed to do the same.

Four years later, Essie Askew applied for a Coors distributorship, and got it. But the expansion tripled the territory her company would have to serve and that required two new trucks and a cooler, which put her $100,000 in debt.

It was a bold gamble, but it paid off.

The year that Askew got the Coors distributorship, Askew Distributing sold 338,000 cases of beer; a year later, 700,000 cases.

Employment has more than doubled, and the firm is in solid financial condition.

Planning to Leave

Most of us would like to *walk* away before we are *carried* away, but none of us has any such assurance. The wise approach is to determine, early on, what to do with the business once you leave it, and there are many ways to deal with that question.

Some people have children who are interested in the business, capable enough to run it, and eager to have the opportunity. Others have employees, relatives, a competitor, or some other investor who would like to take over.

Many entrepreneurs would like to have a say in who runs their company after they leave. Some would even like to stay around for awhile, perhaps in a reduced capacity. Still others would simply prefer to cut the cord and walk away.

The choices are many and sometimes complex. The final decision is an extremely personal one, but we can offer some options, provide some suggestions worth considering, and then allow you to reach you own conclusions.

Possibility 1: Pass the Company to Your Heirs

Not all spouses have the management skills and determination of Joyce Signer or Essie Askew. Besides, in most situations, your spouse will want to retire when you do. Therefore, let's consider your heirs to be primarily the second generation, whether that means your children or some of your nieces and nephews.

Let us also be candid. Statistics prove that less than 30 percent of the family businesses make it to the second generation, and less than half of those make it to a third generation. If the batting average of the first generation is none too good, that of the second generation is even worse.

Looking for a Life of Their Own

Many young people want to pursue careers of their own. They want to be a part of their own generation, not a clone of their parents'. Having been closely associated with the family business for most of their lives, they want a change.

There also are economic realities to be faced. If the family business has grown to a considerable size, it may be more than the children can handle. There will be the temptation to sell out, take the money, and enjoy life. If the business has fared less well, the children may wonder if it can generate as much income as they would like, or if they wouldn't be better off pursuing something else.

Make the Wrong Choice and the Business Could Fold

Even the most devoted parent will realize that blood isn't necessarily as important as brains when it comes to running a successful business. It would serve no purpose to turn over your business to someone who lacks the ability to operate it. It would be more merciful to sell the company and distribute the proceeds than to watch the company deteriorate, and its value vanish.

If the company is incorporated, it can be given to one's heirs in the form of stock *without* turning over the day-to-day operations to them. That way, they can live off the income from the business while someone more competent assumes management.

What Will the Government Allow?

Chicago's Pritzker family has passed along its $3.5-billion empire through a series of more than 1,000 trust funds. Unfortunately, the government has since abolished that means of preserving the family's fortune.

Only $600,000 may now be passed along in your will. Anything over that is taxable (37-percent minimum, 55-percent maximum). But you can give away $10,000 a year, tax free, to as many people as you wish, relatives or otherwise, while you are still alive.

You can put a large estate into a grantor retained income trust today and live off the income for the rest of your life. When the trust expires, the principal and any capital appreciation will pass on to your heirs tax free.

If you are incorporated, you can divide your stock into preferred stock and common shares. The preferred stock, which you retain, has a par value equal to the net worth of the company. The common stock, which you give to your children, will reflect any appreciation in the net worth of the company. In this way, you "freeze" the value of your business and no further appreciation will be taxed to your estate.

"Selling" the Business to Your Children

You can sell the company to your children in installments or by means of an annuity sale.

A *sale by installments* simply means that you agree on a price for the company and specify the period of time over which the payments will be made:

Value of company	$1,000,000
Number of annual payments	20
Annual payment	$50,000

Once all of the payments have been made, the sale is complete.

An *annuity sale* means that you agree on a price for the company and then use a life expectancy table to determine the size of the annual payments:

Value of company	$1,000,000
Life expectancy	11½ years
Annual payment	$86,957

Under the annuity plan, the payments continue as long as you live, even if you live well beyond the projected 11½ years, but they stop as soon as you die, even if you die within the first year.

Under either approach, the business passes to your children immediately and is no longer a part of your taxable estate.

If the Children Are *Really* Young...

What if your children are too young to run a business? Then you might consider creating a testamentary trust, funded with your common stock. Under this arrangement, if you should die, a trustee will run your company until your children reach a specified age (which you establish). At that time, the children can take over the business, if they wish.

Make Your Preference Known

Whatever course you decide on, it will be wise to discuss it with your family and make sure your views coincide with theirs. If not, then some rethinking is in order.

Although you may be able to impose your wishes on your children while you are alive, you can't continue to do so after you have gone. Do your children want to continue operating the company? Do they want the ownership, but not the responsibility of running it? Or would they simply prefer to have the money that can be obtained by selling the business?

Everyone will be happier with your decision if they have had a role in formulating it.

The services of a financial counselor can be extremely valuable. And once you have reached a decision, have a competent lawyer execute the paperwork for you.

Possibility 2: Pass The Company to a Partner or to the Employees

Partners often resolve the question of succession at the very outset. Under the terms of their startup agreement, they specify that, in the event of a death, the survivor is to buy out the interest of the deceased partner. The agreement describes how the value of the company is to be determined and how the survivor is to compensate the heir(s) of the deceased.

Of course, even without such an agreement, partners should be your first thought if you decide to sell your business interest. They already know the business, they have a substantial investment in it, and presumably they have the greatest interest in buying you out. This too can be accomplished in a variety of ways, most of which already have been discussed.

Leveraged Buyout

Increasingly popular these days is a plan for transferring ownership of the company to the employees. One such plan involves a leveraged buyout, in which a group of senior-level employees makes a down payment on the firm and agrees to pay the owner the balance, in installments, from the company's future earnings. If they default on the payments, of course, the company may revert to the original owner.

The leveraged buyout offers a number of advantages:

- It is a relatively inexpensive way for the employees to acquire a business of their own.

- It assures that the company will be run by seasoned, experienced people.

- It provides the new management with a strong incentive to succeed because (a) the company now belongs to them and (b) they must operate the business carefully in order to earn enough money to make the installment payments.

- It provides the seller with some immediate cash plus the income from the installments yet to be paid. (Unless, of course, the buyers have taken out a loan with which to make full payment to the seller. Then the installments go to a bank or other lender, not to the seller.)

Employee Stock Ownership Plan

Another popular plan includes all of the company's employees and is commonly called an employee stock ownership plan (ESOP). This program is notable for its flexibility:

- The owner can prescribe who may and may not qualify to participate, within certain limits.

- The owner can sell as much or as little stock as he or she chooses.

- The owner can use the plan as an incentive to increase employees' efficiency or productivity.

- Such a plan results in an infusion of new capital into the company.

- A company can get a bank loan at below-market interest rates by channeling the loan through the ESOP, and all payments on the loan—both principal and interest—are tax deductible.

- The owner can get a substantial tax break by selling his or her shares to the ESOP—and the owner's heirs may be able to avoid taxes entirely.

Flip back to Family Success Scenario 60 (Chapter 11), and reread the account of Chad Frost's efforts to rehabilitate the family business. An ESOP was one of the techniques that Frost used to finance improvements in the plant and to stimulate greater employee involvement.

_____ **FAMILY SUCCESS SCENARIO 64** _____

LIGHT & POWER PRODUCTIONS, INC.
Scotia, New York

Charles Hanley and George Schubert planned their entire futures around an ESOP when they founded their audiovisual service and events management company.

When they created the firm, Hanley and Schubert signed an agreement to sell the organization to its employees about ten years down the line. They even set the date.

It was a very unusual plan.

Employees would have an option to buy the company, but would not be required to do so. The selling price would be two times retained earnings, which would not exceed $300,000. A generous pension and profit-sharing plan would provide much of the cash that the employees would need for the buyout. The company would be required to buy back the shares owned by anyone who left the firm.

On the specified date, the employees could pay the owners half of the total purchase price and pay the remaining half, plus interest, in installments over the next seven years.

The plan worked beautifully. In an 11-year span, only one employee left the company. One year, to offset unexpectedly high operating expenses, the employees unanimously voted to a 10-percent cut in pay.

The year before the employee buyout, the company produced

$2.5 million in revenues, and had $300,000 in retained earnings. How did Hanley and Schubert make out in the sale?

1. The pair derived an income from the company for 11 years *prior to the sale*.
2. By the time of the sale, the partners had acquired some real estate, including the building in which their company was operating.
3. They had the proceeds from the sale of a subsidiary as well as the parent company, their share of the pension and profit-sharing funds, and deferred income, all worth nearly $1 million apiece.
4. They were offered the opportunity to stay on and manage the business for the company's new owners.

Possibility 3: Take the Company Public

If your company has grown to the point where it meets the requirements of the American or New York Stock Exchanges, and has a track record that will make it attractive to the investing public, you may consider this option.

Such a move requires no elaboration, but it is one that clearly calls for the use of competent financial and legal advisers, able to explain the numerous pros and cons as they relate to your specific situation.

Possibility 4: Sell Out to Another Firm

Once again, there seems to be little need to elaborate on this option. Your company is absorbed by another firm in exchange for cash and/or stock.

Sound legal and financial counsel is needed.

Possibility 5: Sell Out to Venture Capitalists

Venture capitalists are always looking for good properties—particularly those with high growth potential. But many of these firms drive a very hard bargain, and extreme caution is advised.

Be particularly careful as to *what* you sell. Are you selling the company alone or your services along with it? In some cases, you may be obliged to stay on for a specified amount of time; but you also may find that the venture firm has saddled you with severe rules and regulations that will make your job extremely difficult, and that might also affect your financial return on the sale.

Possibility 6: Find a
Business Broker

There are brokers who specialize in buying and selling companies. According to some calculations, such firms sell about 75,000 companies each year, most of them for less than $300,000.

Once more, extreme caution is advisable. Some brokers approach an owner saying that they have a prospective buyer for the company when, in fact, they do not. If the owner shows an interest in selling, then the broker will go out to hunt for a buyer.

This can waste a lot of the owner's time, raise some false hopes, and possibly disrupt normal business operations. If word that the owner is "selling out" spreads to the business' suppliers and customers, it can cause additional problems. Your competitors — or your employees — may also get wind of it.

Some brokers charge the seller a packaging fee to develop the company's profile and evaluate its worth. These fees can range from $200 to $20,000, and must be paid up front, whether the broker manages to sell the company or not.

In addition, the broker will charge a commission if a buyer is located, and this can range from 10 to 12 percent, with a minimum of $5,000 to $10,000. (Occasionally, brokers will deduct their packaging fee from the commission if a sale is made. Be sure to establish this with the broker before you enter into an agreement.)

Select a broker carefully. Talk to others who have used their services. Study the broker's track record. If they average below 50 percent on listings that they have carried for six months or a year, then look further.

Finally, the Choice Is Up to You

In the final analysis, the process of letting go is usually a traumatic experience.

How could it be otherwise? You gave birth to the company, and nurtured it like one of your children. You worried about its financial health and growth. In return, it took care of you as well — paid for the house and car, put the kids through school, made it possible for you to get where you are today.

In letting go, the important thing isn't *how* you do it or *when* you do it, but that *you will be happy with the outcome.*

Chapter 12 Checkup

Set Your Objectives Now

1. List your preretirement goals:

   Targeted retirement date   _____
   Age at retirement   _____ years
   Cash value of all assets $ _____
   Amount of monthly income $ _____
      Source   _____

2. Rate each of the following possibilities according to your personal preference:

   Retaining the company
      Using other management   _____
      Via your stock holdings   _____
   Turning the company over to others
      Your children   _____
      Other relatives   _____
      A partner   _____
      The employees   _____
   Selling the company
      Outright   _____
      In installments   _____

Study these choices. Compare what you want to have for your retirement as far as financial security is concerned, along with your options regarding the future management of the company.

Which of the latter will be most likely to provide for a secure retirement?

What do you need to do *now* to put yourself in position for retirement when your targeted retirement date comes around?

How will your decisions be received by your children, your other relatives, your partner(s), and the employees? Have you discussed it with them?

Index